CHURCHES OF BEDFORDSHIRE

JOHN JACKSON

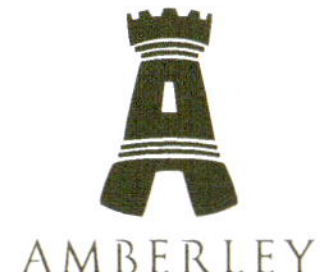

AMBERLEY

This edition first published 2024

Amberley Publishing
The Hill, Stroud
Gloucestershire GL5 4EP

www.amberley-books.com

British Library Cataloguing in Publication Data.
A catalogue record for this book is available from the British Library.

ISBN 978 1 3981 1821 8 (print)
ISBN 978 1 3981 1822 5 (ebook)

Typesetting by SJmagic DESIGN SERVICES, India.
Printed in Great Britain.

CONTENTS

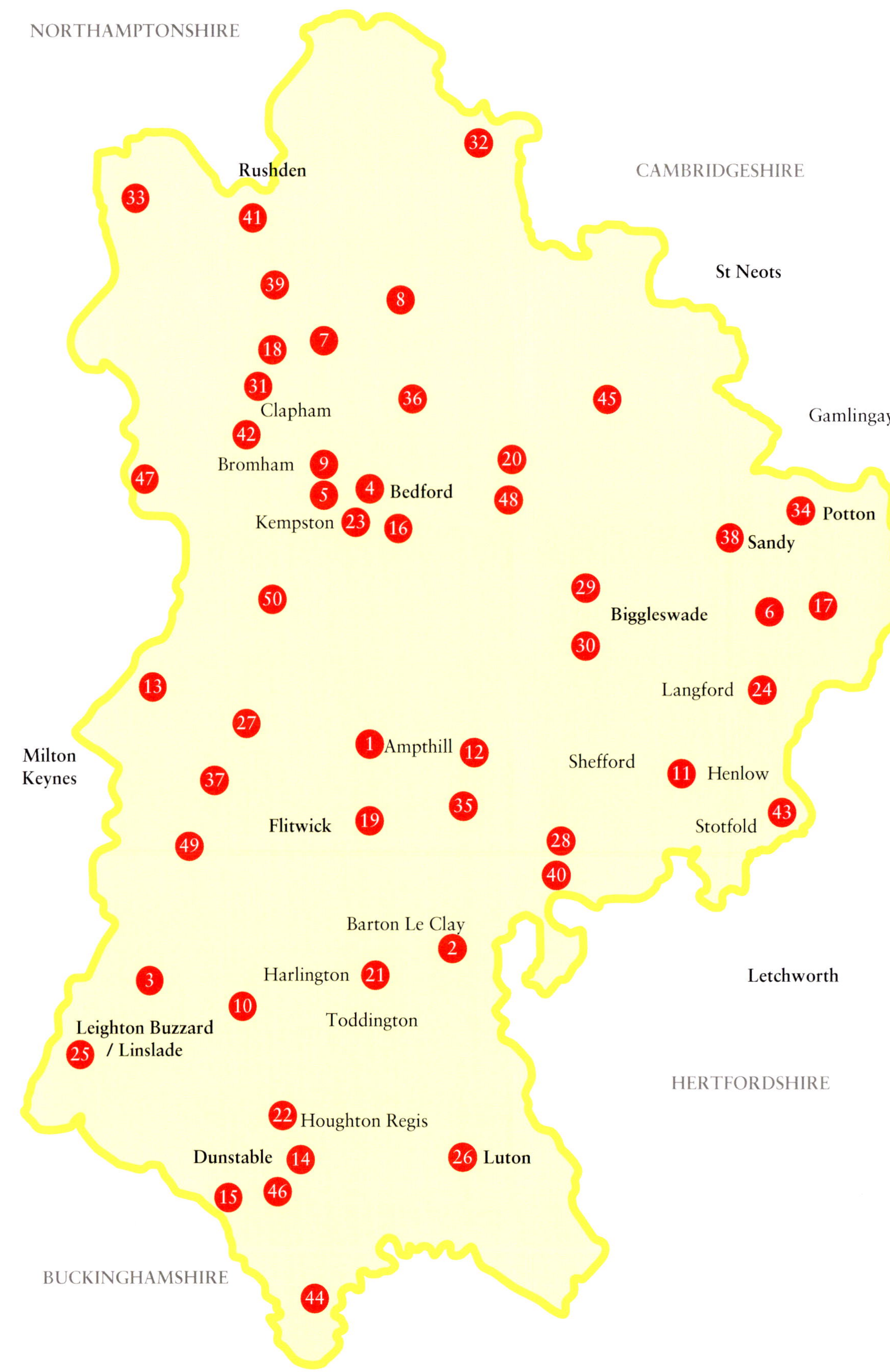

NORTHAMPTONSHIRE
CAMBRIDGESHIRE
St Neots
Rushden
Gamlingay
Clapham
Bromham
Bedford
Kempston
Potton
Sandy
Biggleswade
Langford
Milton Keynes
Ampthill
Shefford
Henlow
Flitwick
Stotfold
Barton Le Clay
Letchworth
Harlington
Toddington
Leighton Buzzard / Linslade
HERTFORDSHIRE
Houghton Regis
Dunstable
Luton
BUCKINGHAMSHIRE

Introduction

The county of Bedfordshire is one of England's smallest, occupying an area of under 500 square miles. Around 750,000 residents call the county their home, with approximately half of them living in the two largest urban areas, Luton and Bedford, the historic county town.

The county sees a number of important roads passing through its borders, notably the A1, A5 and A6. To these can be added the M1, which opened at the end of the 1950s, bringing the number of north to south arteries running through the county to four. To many long-distance travellers, that is the extent of their knowledge of the county, which is a shame as the county is worthy of further exploration and, in this publication, we hope to show why, as we explore the area through its churches, of which there are around 150.

Several years ago, myself and Jenny Jackson, together with Jenny's father, John Sumner, embarked on a quest to explore these churches in more detail. John Sumner has lived the majority of his ninety-two years within the county. My recent books include a detailed look at the railways of Bedfordshire in the twenty-first century, and now it is local churches that have been put under the spotlight.

Having visited all of the parish churches in the county, our selection process was a difficult one. Our aim was to bring to life the stories attached to around fifty of them. In arriving at our final selection, we wanted to reflect our belief that the churches' architecture is but one aspect of their interest. After all, a church is as much about its people and every one of the churches we have chosen provides an insight to those who have shaped Bedfordshire's history from many centuries ago to the present day.

Our journey around the county inevitably includes references to John Bunyan, perhaps Bedfordshire's most famous son. One of the most oppressed Nonconformists he may have been, but it was at Elstow Abbey that he was brought for baptism, and, later, to receive communion. Other famous Bedfordshire residents include Samuel Whitbread, the eighteenth-century brewer and politician whose family have close connections to the church at Cardington. St Andrew's Church in Biggleswade is the final resting place of Mary Tealby. Perhaps, Mary is not so well known but her place in history is guaranteed as the founder of Battersea Dogs Home. Our in-depth look at the churches of Bedfordshire uncovered a vast array of these human stories, ranging from household names to the almost anonymous.

We hope that, on the pages that follow, you enjoy our selection of these churches, their buildings and their people, as much as we have enjoyed compiling them.

1. Ampthill, St Andrew the Apostle

The town of Ampthill in Central Bedfordshire lies 7 miles south of Bedford, between the county town and Luton. Today, it has a population of around 8,000.

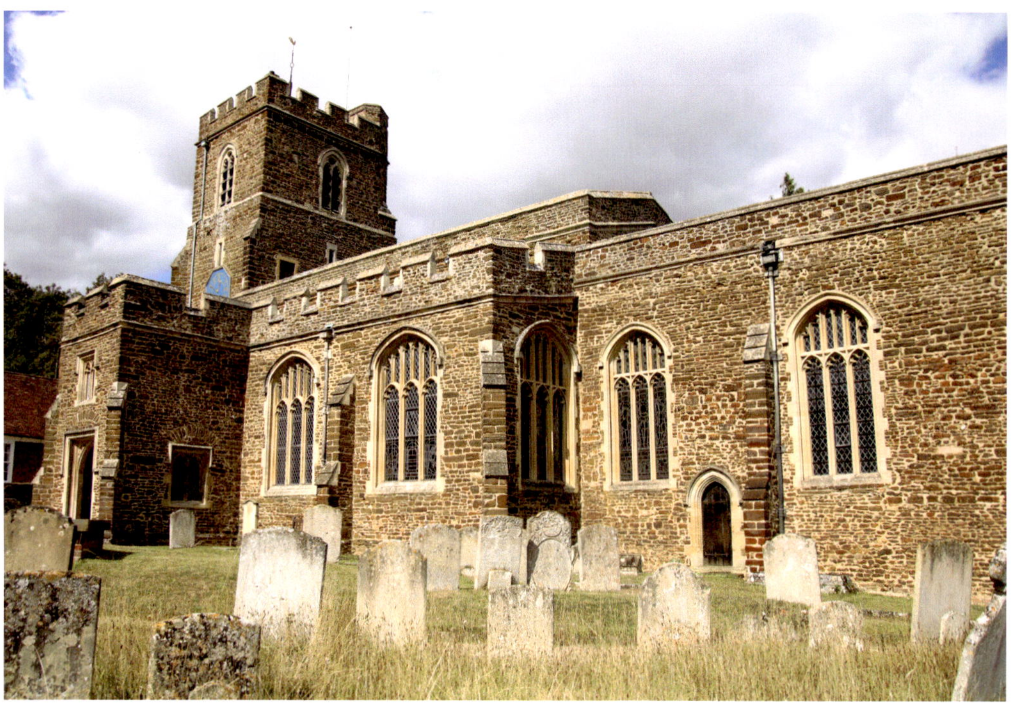

Ampthill Church.

The church of St Andrew the Apostle is situated in the cul-de-sac of Rectory Lane in the northeast corner of the town, just off Church Street, leading to Maulden.

The original foundations date from the thirteenth century but the church we see today is largely fourteenth and fifteenth century. It was Sir John Cornwall, a soldier and leader who was a hero of the Battle of Agincourt (1415) in the Hundred Years' War, who paid for the current church's enlargement.

The church is entered via the distinctive two-storey porch on the south side. The upper storey has seen a variety of usage including by visiting clergy and as general 'office' space. Another feature of note within the church is the gallery above the font. The font is housed at the base of the tower.

The church has maintained its links with its 600 years of history with a modern-day stained-glass window, dating from 1982. This window is a modern replacement, depicting Sir John Cornwall and his wife, Princess Elizabeth of Lancaster. Elizabeth was the sister of Henry IV and was known as something of a royal rebel. Sir John was, in fact, her third husband. The window serves as an ongoing reminder of this local national hero's contribution in the building of the church.

Another window in the church, also in the chancel, is dedicated in memory of local parishioner Mrs T. Wingfield. The Wingfield family home was at nearby Ampthill House, demolished in the 1950s. The churchyard contains the Wingfield family grave, guarded over by the 'Wingfield Angel'.

In common with all churches, ongoing restoration work requires many fundraising activities and St Andrew the Apostle is no exception. A more ingenious recent example was the raising of over £6,000 by the local rector, who sky dived over Salisbury Plain in 2023.

St Andrew the Apostle in Ampthill forms a benefice with St Michael's at Millbrook and St Lawrence's in Steppingley.

2. BARTON-LE-CLAY, ST NICHOLAS

With a population of around 5,000, the large village of Barton-le-Clay is situated in the southeast of Bedfordshire, close to the Hertfordshire border. The church and its associated buildings were formerly in the separate hamlet of Church End but are, today, part of the main village. The Grade I church of St Nicholas is located in a cul-de-sac south from the B655, the road from Barton to Hitchin.

Most of the present church dates back to the thirteenth and fourteenth centuries, although like many churches it is mentioned in the Domesday Book and some of the masonry dates to the twelfth century. On approaching the church, one cannot fail to be impressed by the fifteenth-century tower. It is decorated in a distinctive chequerboard style and houses eight bells, three of which date from the seventeenth and eighteenth centuries.

On entering the church, the eye is drawn to its wooden roof. The north aisle has carved figures of the twelve apostles. Further investigation leads us to the font, which was recut in the fifteenth century. The distinctive rope mould of the rim,

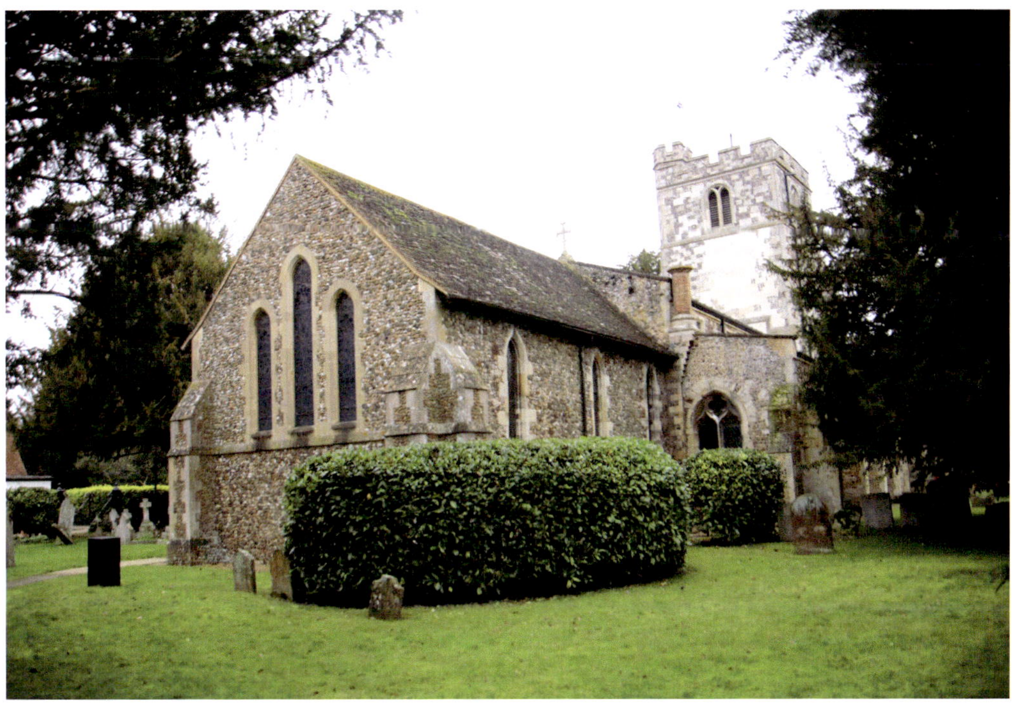

Barton-le-Clay Church.

and perhaps the fluted band, are twelfth-century originals. Around the time of the church restoration work in the 1870s and 1880s, a stained-glass east window was unveiled in commemoration of the then queen, Victoria.

Unfortunately, the time of our visit did not coincide with either the annual Christmas Tree Festival, now well established for over twenty years, or the blooming of the handkerchief tree within its churchyard.

Today, the benefice contains three churches. The church of St Nicholas in Barton-le-Clay is joined with St Margaret's Church at Higham Gobion and St Faith's at Hexton. The latter village lies over the county border in Hertfordshire. The fourteenth-century church at Higham Gobion serves a very small community of just a few houses, forming part of the civil parish of Shillington since the mid-1980s.

3. BATTLESDEN, ST PETER AND ALL SAINTS

The tiny community of Battlesden lies between Dunstable and Milton Keynes, just to the north of the A5. Together with the nearby hamlet of Potsgrove, the two remote communities have a combined population of fewer than 100.

Although the church of St Peter and All Saints is hard to find, the effort is rewarding. It lies a mile and a half up a rural, single-track lane off the A4012 road. The church stands in what was the grounds of Battlesden House. This sixteenth-century house was demolished and cleared after the Second World War.

The simply designed church, like many others, has timeline anomalies, not least because the medieval church appears to pre-date the house itself. Consisting of an embattled nave and chancel, the church tower has been built on the nave's

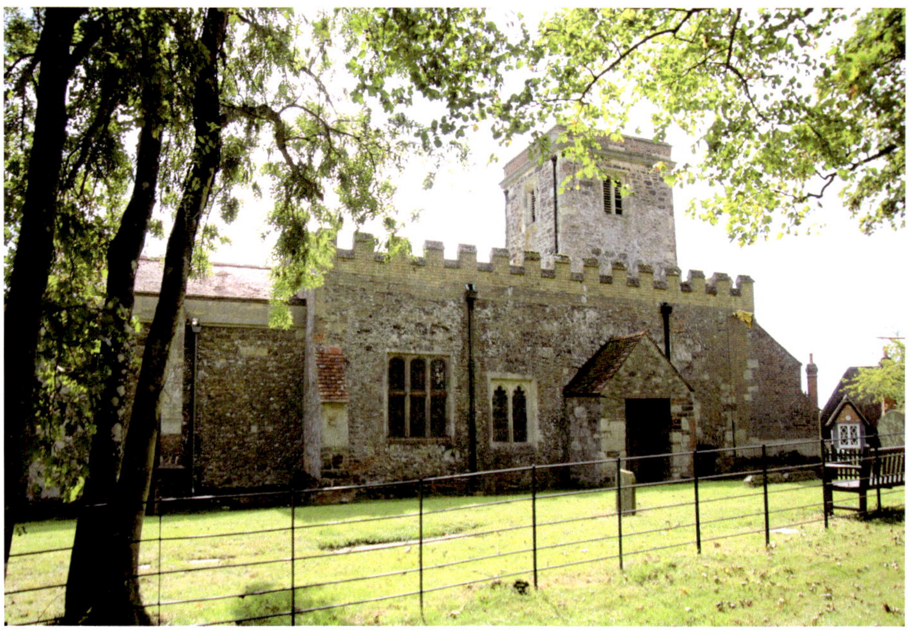

Battlesden Church.

southwest corner. The church is entered through a small porch and north doorway. Probably the most impressive feature inside the church is the font, which dates back to the twelfth century. It is shaped like a drum with leaf carving and has an impressive conical-shaped wooden cover.

The annals of history tell the church's story of an organ-playing boy who saw a monk in a brown habit at the same time as the verger and a parishioner reported seeing a man in a brown coat. The nearest monks were at Woburn Abbey and wore white habits due to being Cistercian. A more recent incident at the turn of the millennium records a child being frightened by something and crying whilst hiding in a corner of the church. It is from these documented experiences that the church has gained a reputation for being haunted.

The church of St Peter and All Saints, Battlesden, is part of the Woburn benefice. This benefice includes St Mary's, Woburn; St Peter's, Milton Bryan; St John the Baptist, Eversholt; and St Mary's Potsgrove and Battlesden. The Woburn benefice was created in 1980 with the trustees of the Woburn estate as its patron. Differing from the others in the benefice, Battlesden with Potsgrove covers the largest land area but with by far the fewest parishioners.

St Peter and All Saints is the centre for active worship for both Battlesden and Potsgrove. It has a monthly service, the second Sunday in the month, with attendances increasing markedly since Covid with a regular congregation of around twenty. This tight-knit community share the responsibility for running the church and looking out for each other.

4. BEDFORD, ST PAUL

Located in the very heart of Bedford town centre, St Paul's is the largest church in the entire county. Its magnificent spire dominates the town, on a site that has seen worship for more than a millennium. St Paul's Church has a nave and aisles of approximately equal height and is often referred to as a hall church. It blends the modern with the medieval, with many features dating back to the Middle Ages. Its spire dates from the eighteenth century and replaced the original fourteenth-century structure. It is, in fact, a cathedral by any other name.

It came to prominence during the darkest hours of the Second World War, and it was chosen by the BBC to host its daily worship during these war years. The 1941 National Day of Prayer, on 7 September that year, was also broadcast from here, with the then Archbishop of Canterbury leading the worship to an audience across the UK and the wider world.

This period of the church's notoriety is marked by the inscription on the floor of the chapel's entrance, which reads 'The BBC broadcast the Christian message from this chapel 1941–1945 in the darkness of war: Nation shall speak peace unto nation. They shall beat their swords into ploughshares. Hope through reconciliation. Forgiveness through understanding. Peace.'

The church's interior contains both a memorial to Simon de Beauchamp, founder of Newnham Priory, and to Sir William Harpur, a former Lord Mayor of London. This local Bedford merchant, who was London's mayor in 1561, was knighted a year later. Both he and his wife Alice never forgot their Bedford roots. The pair of them are well known locally for their charitable work, in particular

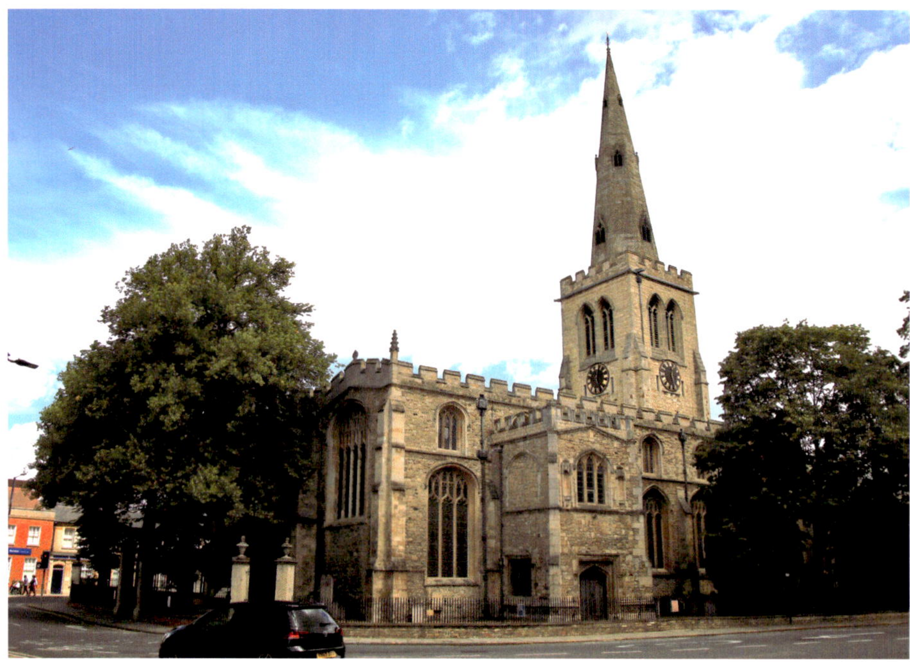

Bedford, St Paul's Church.

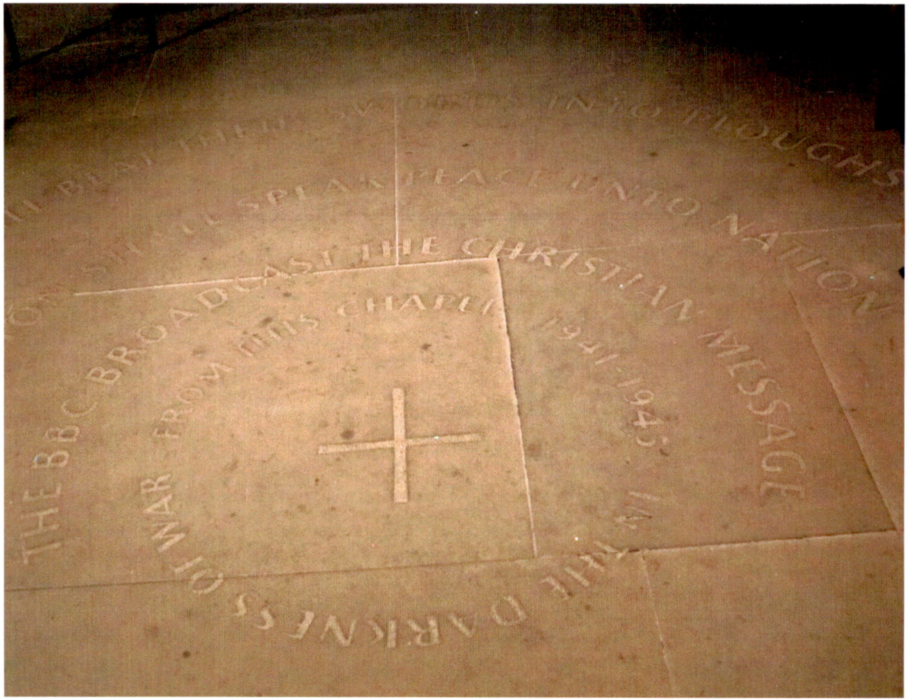

BBC Wartime message, St Paul's Church.

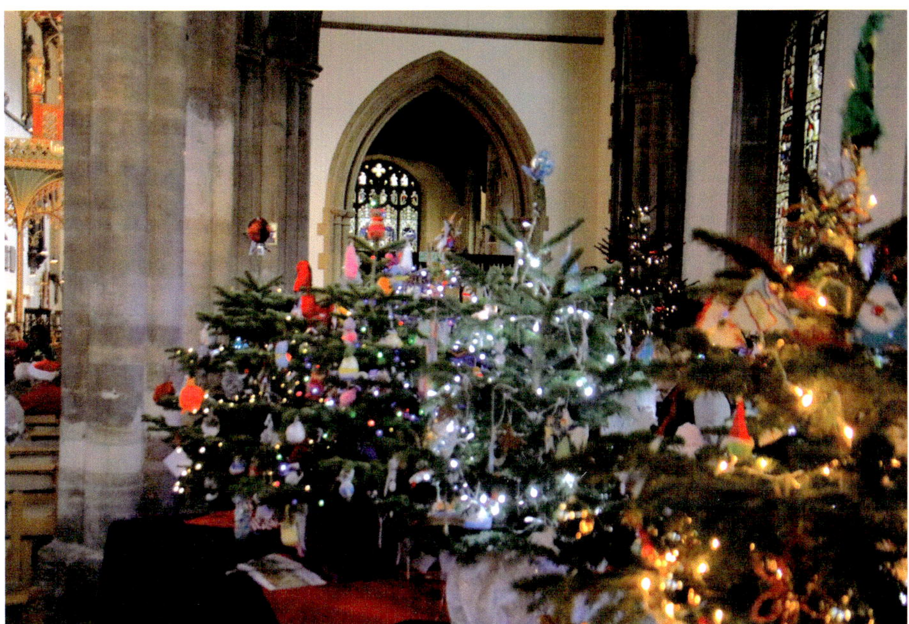

Christmas Tree Festival, St Paul's Church.

with regard to education. To this day, the trust founded in their names continues to support local education and leisure.

Both John Bunyan and John Wesley, founder of the Methodist movement, are likely to have preached from the church's impressive stone pulpit which, although no longer in use, retains its place in this church's history.

St Paul's also plays host to a variety of concerts and other events throughout the year. It is particularly well known for its Christmas Tree Festival. Since 2000, each December the church houses a number of decorated Christmas trees for locals to admire, with funds raised being used in part to support the local hospital's charity. More than sixty trees were on display in 2022, attracting thousands of visitors over the five-day event, raising over £20,000.

5. BIDDENHAM, ST JAMES

The village of Biddenham lies in a bend on the River Great Ouse around 2 miles to the west of the town of Bedford itself. Today, the church serves the parishes of Biddenham and nearby Great Denham, the latter community being created a parish in its own right as recently as 2007.

There has been a settlement here since Roman times, with a significant archaeological find of Stone Age implements made close to the church in the mid-nineteenth century. Their importance was such that they are now housed in the British Museum.

The church's history dates back to the eleventh or twelfth centuries, when the building was likely a wooden structure. The stone building we see today has gradually evolved over the centuries as the local area it served both grew and

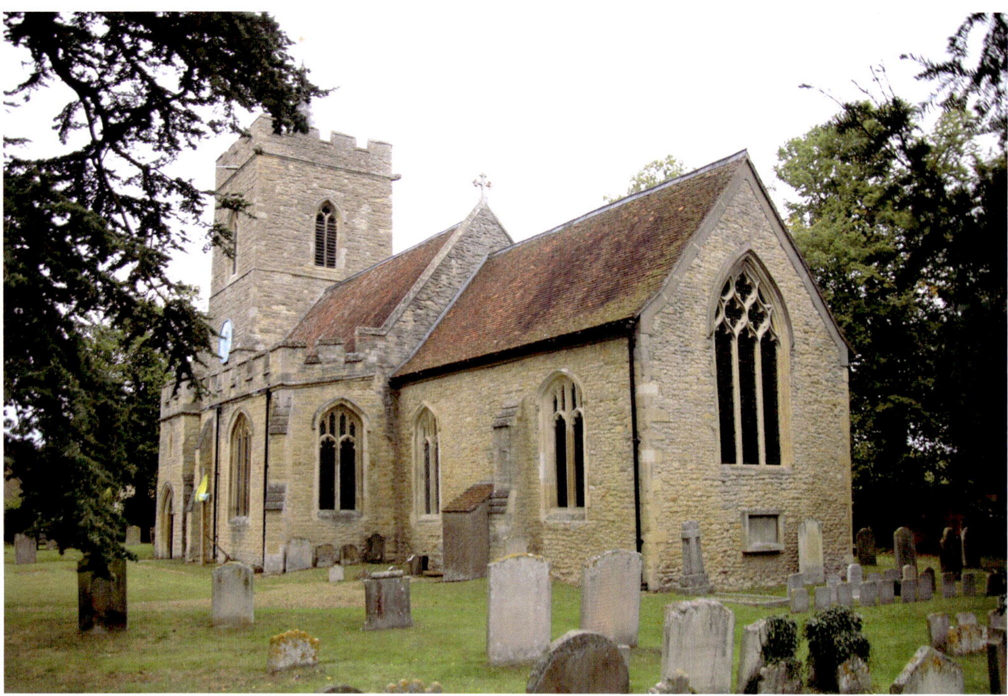

Biddenham Church.

prospered. An example of this is that the lower part of the tower dates from the thirteenth century, whilst the upper was added in the fifteenth century.

The Botelers and the Dwyves were two local wealthy families who paid for the south aisle in the early sixteenth century, as well as founding a charity to assist the poor. Space was still at a premium for centuries later, with a much-needed new vestry being constructed as recently as the 1970s using funds raised by local parishioners.

In the same century, a memorial window was added in memory of Sir John Howard. He was a well-known local dignitary, serving as High Sherriff of Bedfordshire in the 1770s, spending much of his life campaigning for prison reforms. He died in Kherson, in what is now Ukraine.

At the turn of the twenty-first century, a millennium window was commissioned, depicting life in the village. Local community involvement continues to this day. James Burston, for example, a teacher at Bedford Modern School for around twenty years, crafted a Processional Cross and donated it to St James' Church.

Amongst the church's more historic treasures are a leather-bound bible, notably written in English, and prayer book, the former published in 1739 and the latter in 1748. It was only 100 years or so earlier than this that people, or at least those able to read, were permitted to use the bible. Often, the only copies available were in the hands of the church's priest, who may also have been illiterate.

The church of St James, Biddenham, is in a benefice with All Saints Church in Kempston.

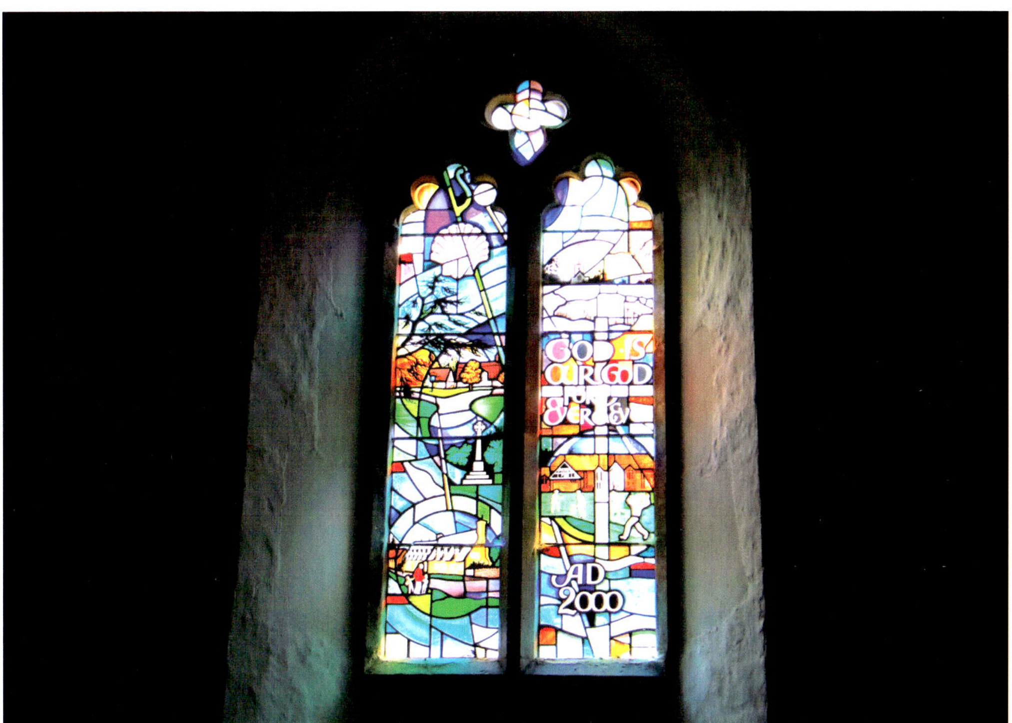

Millennium window, Biddenham.

6. BIGGLESWADE, ST ANDREW

Biggleswade is a quaint market town situated on the River Ivel and adjacent to the main A1 road. It is just over 10 miles southeast of Bedford and 45 miles north of London. The town's population is around 22,000 today.

The church is dedicated to St Andrew and is an ancient holy structure. The church's records state the first vicar was appointed in 1276, although it is likely there was a place of worship preceding the vicar's appointment. During the fourteenth century the church was enlarged considerably. In fact, the extended places can be seen by looking up at the ceiling today, where double beams indicate the joins.

One of the most important people in St Andrew's Church's history is John Rudying. He was the Archdeacon of Bedford in 1467 and paid for the construction of the chancel, making it longer and higher than the nave. In recognition of his contribution, his coat of arms was carved on some antique wooden stalls in the north aisle.

In the seventeenth century, the church suffered from lack of restoration; its tower and two aisles collapsed. As its congregation grew, so did the renovation work. The original tower was rebuilt in 1720 and this now houses a peal of five bells dating from 1721 to 1806. The window in the south aisle is very personal to St Andrew's as it commemorates the Biggleswade fire of 1785 in which much

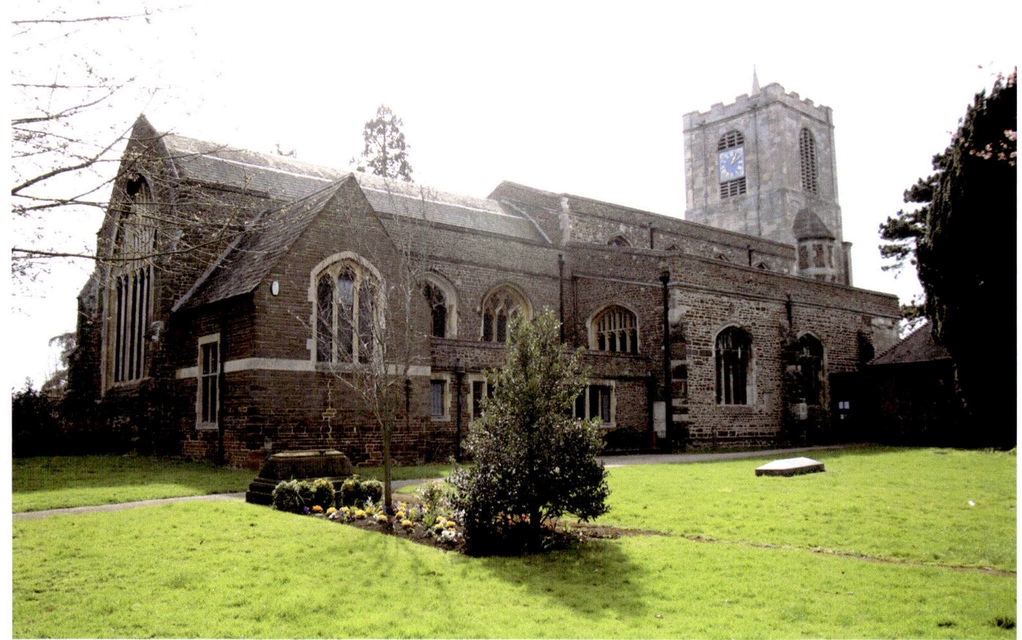

Biggleswade Church.

of the town was destroyed. The window was donated by a parishioner in 1951 in memory of his wife.

Unlike many churches, St Andrew's is in very good condition. This is mainly due to the Friends of St Andrew's Association who have financed the restoration of the tower, south porch, bells, organ, tower clock and have created a disabled access through the chapterhouse.

7. Bletsoe, St Mary

The village of Bletsoe, with a population of around 250, lies to the east of the main A6 Bedford to Rushden Road. The church of St Mary is to be found at the village's heart. Together with All Saints Church in Riseley, St Mary's forms the benefice of Riseley with Bletsoe.

Bletsoe church takes an unusual shape, in two respects. Firstly, the tower is at the church's centre with the north and south transepts, nave and chancel radiating from its centre. Secondly, the north transept and chancel are slightly out of alignment compared to the rest of the building.

Whilst a Saxon predecessor is likely, the Norman structure dates from the eleventh century, with evidence of the church's expansion in the thirteenth and fourteenth centuries as the village population grew.

Peering through the church's lychgate, one can't help but be impressed by just how well maintained the site is given the village's comparatively small population. Above the lychgate is an inscription, 'I am the resurrection and the life'. A plaque on the gatepost proudly boasts the church's 900 years of Norman heritage, with inclusion

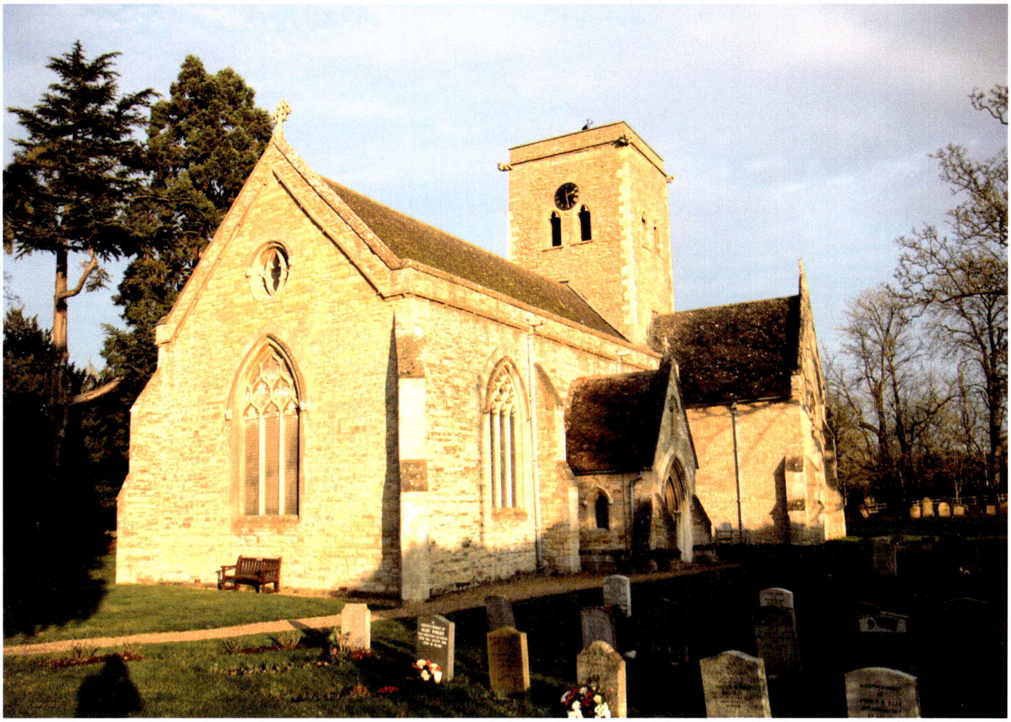

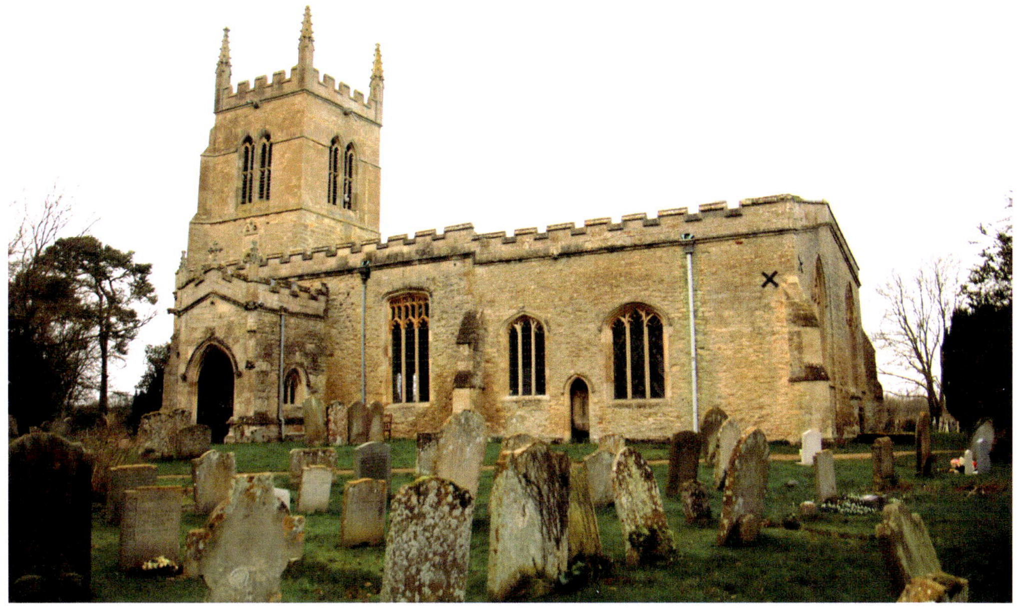

Bletsoe Church.

Riseley Church.

in the Domesday Book of 1086. The parishioners' obvious pride also extends to the church's interior, with a modern well-kept ambience embracing its older artefacts.

Stepping inside the church, the St John family connection is immediately evident with the elaborate alabaster memorial to Sir John St John, his wife and nine children being the first feature to catch the eye. Sir John was a kinsman of Henry VIII, and both were brought up by Margaret Beaufort, the grandmother of Henry VIII, who lived nearby at Bletsoe Castle.

This memorial was moved from the north transept to its present site in the mid-1970s. Amongst the many features reflecting the church's age, the roll of rectors dates back to 1222, commencing with Nicholas de Eston through to the start of this century.

St Mary's sister church is found in the nearby village of Riseley, which is much larger, boasting a population of over 1,200. The church of All Saints is located at the end of Church Lane to the north of Riseley village. The oldest part of this church is the south wall of the south aisle which dates back to the twelfth century.

In a similar way to St Mary's at Bletsoe, a list of rectors and vicars is on display, commencing with Fulco de Monte Acuto, the first rector in 1224. After him, all others are vicars.

8. BOLNHURST, ST DUNSTAN

Bolnhurst is situated 7 miles out of Bedford on the B660, which leads to Kimbolton. St Dunstan's Church is set in an isolated position around a mile to the southwest of the village on the road to Thurleigh. Its remote position is due to the 1348 Black Death destroying the original medieval village of Bolnhurst.

The church is named after St Dunstan who was the Bishop of Worcester and London before becoming Archbishop of Canterbury towards the end of the tenth century. The present church succeeds an older building which was first documented in 1162.

St Dunstan's looks to be built of large square-edged, smooth-facing blocks. This, however, is just a dressing to the – common in these parts – coursed limestone rubble. One enters the church via the south porch which has an elaborate inner door standing between two pointed buttresses and carved faces.

The original thirteenth-century chancel has been renovated and the arch dates to the fourteenth century. The fifteenth-century chancel screen is still in place, as are some of the pews from the same period. Most of the walls inside the church are stone. On the north wall, opposite the door, plaster remains and a faded medieval wall painting of St Christopher and the Christ child is visible.

Today, Bolnhurst forms a benefice known as the 'WCR' with St Nicholas, Wilden; St Denys, Colmsworth; All Saints, Ravensden; and St Mary the Virgin, Keysoe. Bolnhurst and Keysoe form a civil parish with a combined population of approximately 700.

St Mary the Virgin church in Keysoe recalls a fascinating legend within its social history. In 1718, William Dickens, a builder, was working on the steeple when he fell. The legend says he recited a prayer during his fall and was miraculously saved. It was thought that his fall was caused by a rival builder who cut the rope which suspended the chair that William Dickens was sat upon whilst hanging

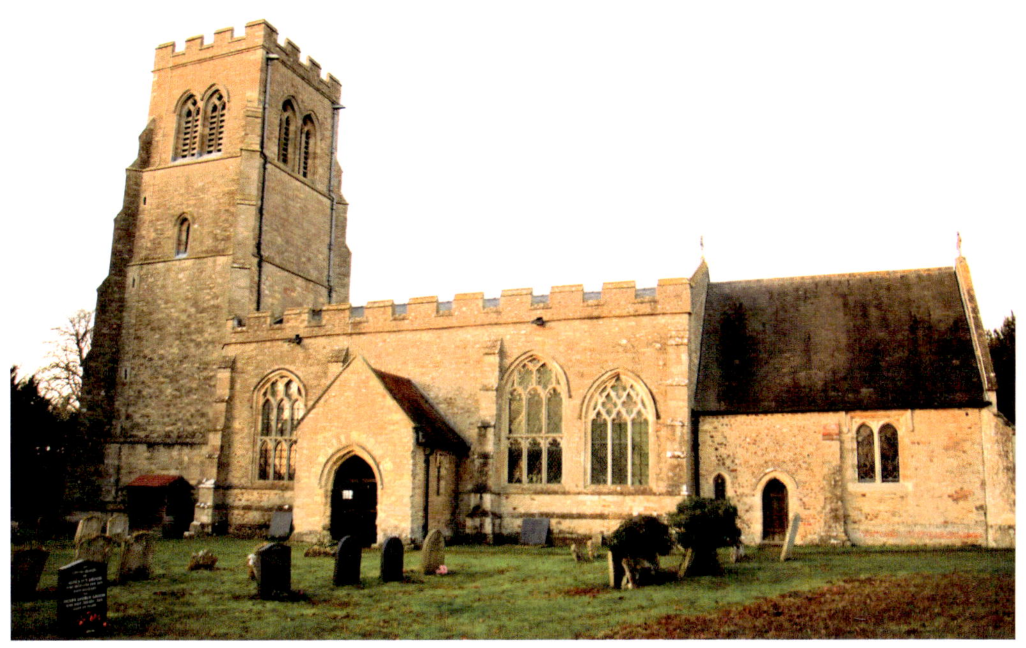

Above: Bolnhurst Church.

Right: Keysoe Church.

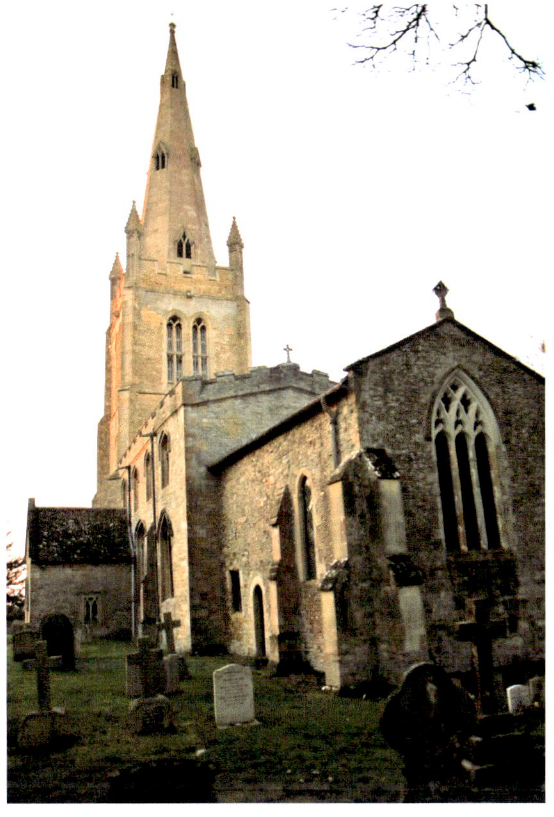

from the spire. This could not be proven but remains on record. The legend goes on to tell how, soon after, the rival builder was admiring his own workmanship on a stack of chimneys when the work crumbled and the builder fell to his death. There is still an old stone at the church which, although weathered, keeps this intriguing legend alive.

9. Bromham, St Owen

The village of Bromham lies 3 miles to the west of Bedford, entered via a distinctive bridge of twenty-six arches over the River Great Ouse. There is local evidence suggesting human existence in the immediate area back around 50 BC. Today, the village has a population of approximately 5,000.

Whilst most parish churches are located at the very heart of the villages they serve, Bromham is an exception with the church standing somewhat isolated within what used to be the parkland of Bromham Hall. Today, the church is reached by a single-track lane across this open parkland, reminding the visitor that it was once on a medieval trading route used by merchants on foot and horseback.

The current building dates from the thirteenth century, although there is evidence of a place of worship being here for almost a thousand years. In medieval times, village dwellings would have been closer to the church. These have since disappeared with newer properties forming the village outside the estate boundaries.

The church is named after the seventh-century French saint Owen (or Ouen), and is believed to be one of only two in this country so named. In early records it

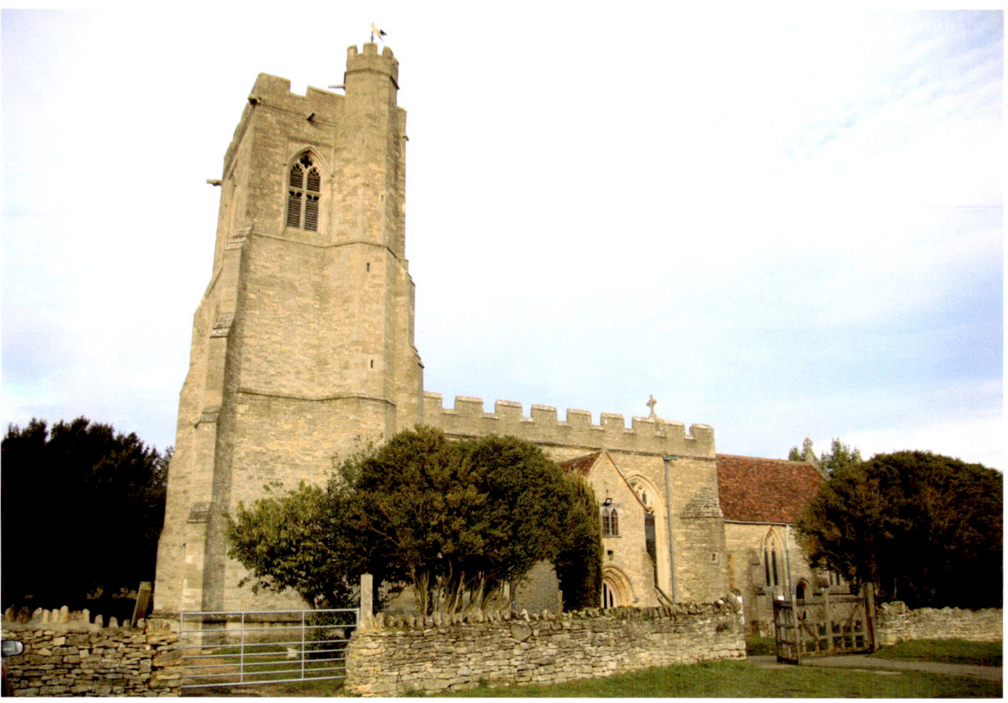

Bromham Church.

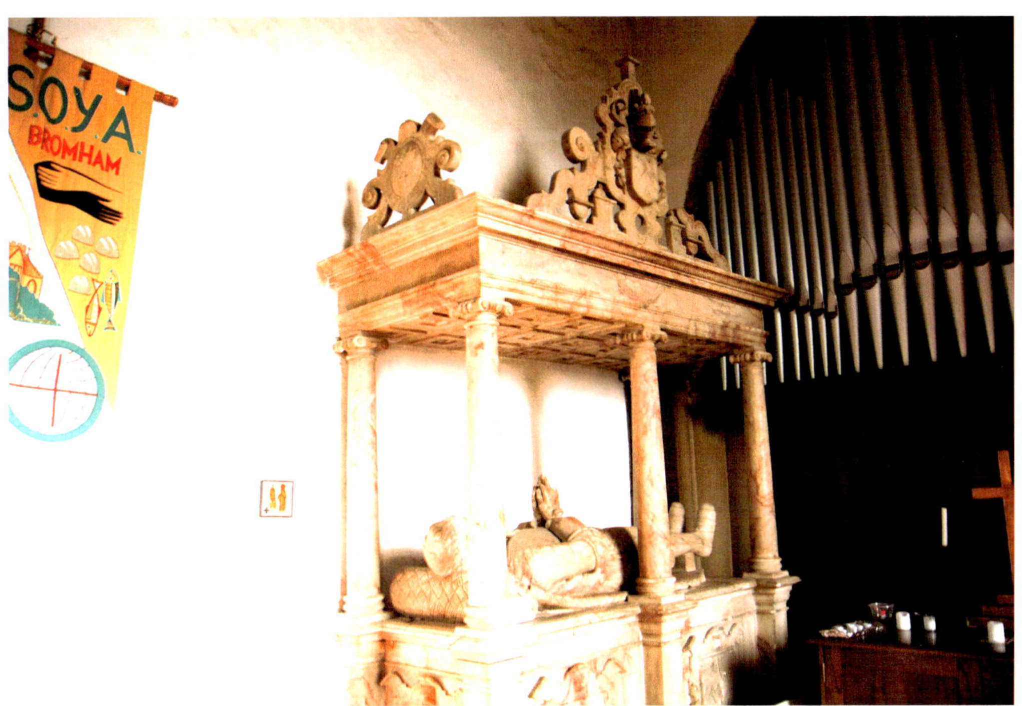

Sir Lewis Dyve tomb, Bromham.

was shown as St Andrew's and the reason for the apparent name change has been lost in the annals of history.

On entering the church, one is greeted by a pleasant mix of both ancient and modern. The modern chairs have replaced older pews, and an extension providing kitchen, toilets and meeting room has been sympathetically incorporated, of which both vicar and parishioners were justifiably proud. The eye is drawn to the pipe organ and the large alabaster tomb of Sir Lewis Dyve, of Bromham Hall, dating back to the turn of the seventeenth century.

The Dyve family subsequently sold the estate to the Trevor family, who also had a long association with Bromham church. This included the donation of books to the church library back in 1740. This was originally housed in the upper storey of the two-storey south porch. These books have since been removed to Canon's Ashby, Northamptonshire, where they remain on permanent loan in the care of the National Trust.

St Owen's Church in Bromham forms a benefice with St Mary's in Oakley and St Leonard's in Stagsden.

10. Chalgrave, All Saints

Chalgrave is a picturesque village near Toddington. It lies 4 miles northwest of Dunstable and 6 miles northeast of Leighton Buzzard, close to the Buckinghamshire border. The hamlet has a population of around 500.

All Saints Church is quite isolated, set high up on a hill, surrounded by trees, to the east of the A5120 road which links Toddington to Houghton Regis, between the A5 and M1.

The earliest record of the church in Chalgrave dates back to the twelfth century. It originally stood adjacent to Chalgrave Castle – hence its hillside position away from the village. The original church was given to the monks of Dunstable Priory in 1185. The priory built a new church in 1219, and many of the thirteenth-century features can still be seen in the structure today.

From the outside of the church there is nothing remarkable; in fact, it looks disproportionate. The chequered tower made of flint and Totternhoe clunch, typical for this area, has been truncated. A gale in the late 1880s blew down the top of the tower, making a hole in the roof. For the best part of fifty years, the church remained closed until it was repaired in 1931. It now has a modern parapet. Even though the tower resembles nothing of its former glory, it still contains the original three bells which are fixed and hammer chimed.

Inside the church, it is rich in interest. It has an ancient feel and is remarkably unrestored. During the 1930s, wall paintings were discovered under five coats of plaster. Although they are damaged, these are considered to be some of the best thirteenth-century surviving wall paintings. It is thought that they depict the twelve apostles. They are almost life-sized and appear in niches around the church.

This historical wall art is somewhat overshadowed by latter-day paintings of texts from the Bible, crests, shields, memorials and two impressive tombs. One

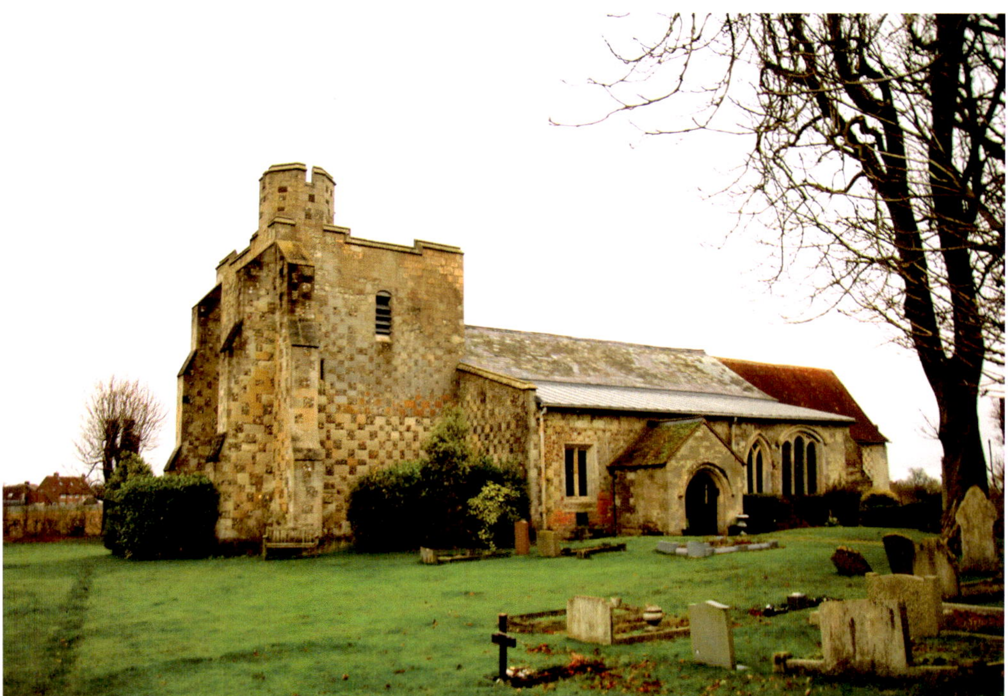

Chalgrave Church.

could spend all day absorbed by the years of history displayed in All Saints Church.

This church is in a benefice with St George's at Toddington.

11. CLIFTON, ALL SAINTS

The village of Clifton, with a population of around 2,800, is in the valley of the River Ivel. Its recent growth is due, in part, to its proximity to Arlesey railway station and being a popular commuter route into London.

All Saint's Church, built approximately 700 years ago in the fourteenth and fifteenth centuries, has been heavily restored in the nineteenth century. That said, the earliest recorded rector dates as far back as 1202. The church is located on Church Street on the road from the village towards Stanford.

The embattled church tower rises to a height of 60 feet. Its distinctive fifteenth-century gargoyles were designed to throw collected rainwater clear of the church walls. Legend has it that this was to serve as a reminder that all those who enter should leave their human vices and sins outside!

Within the church are many interesting features. One immediately sees the stained glass of the impressive east window, which depicts the Ascension, as designed by Reginald Farrar-Bell in 1951. The substantial reredos beneath this window shows the Crucifixion, with the women, together with the apostles Peter and Paul, standing alongside.

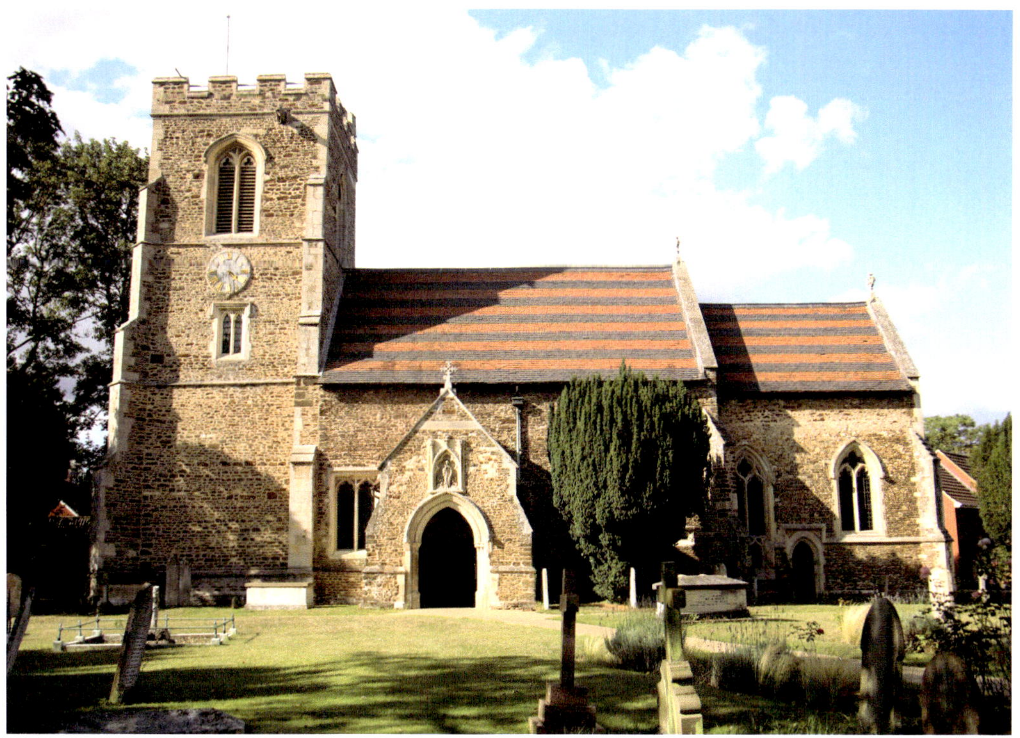

Clifton Church.

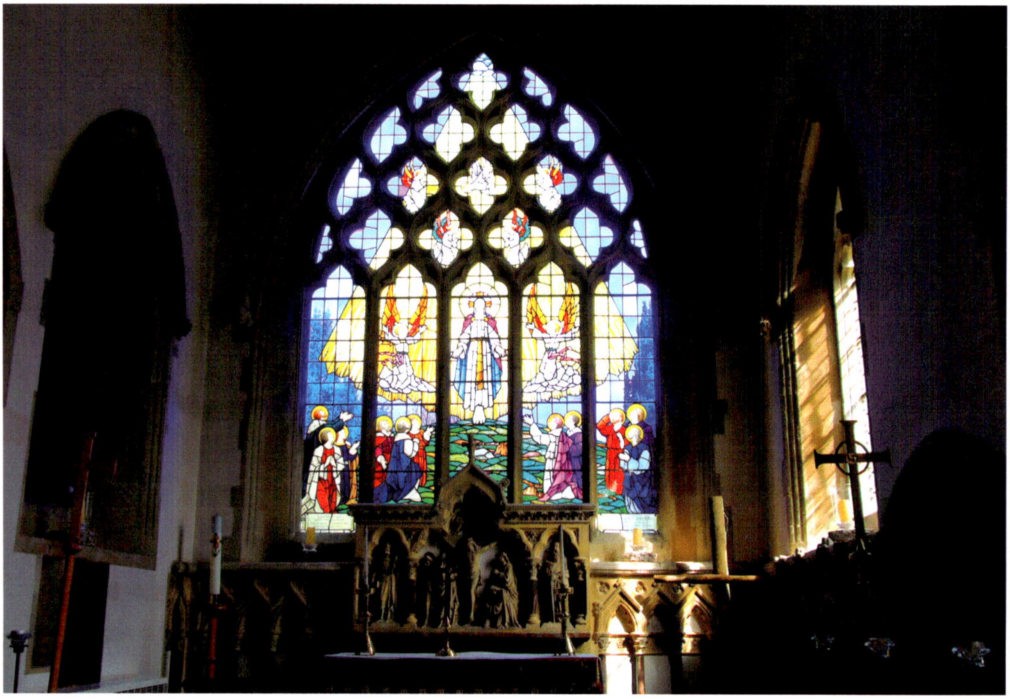

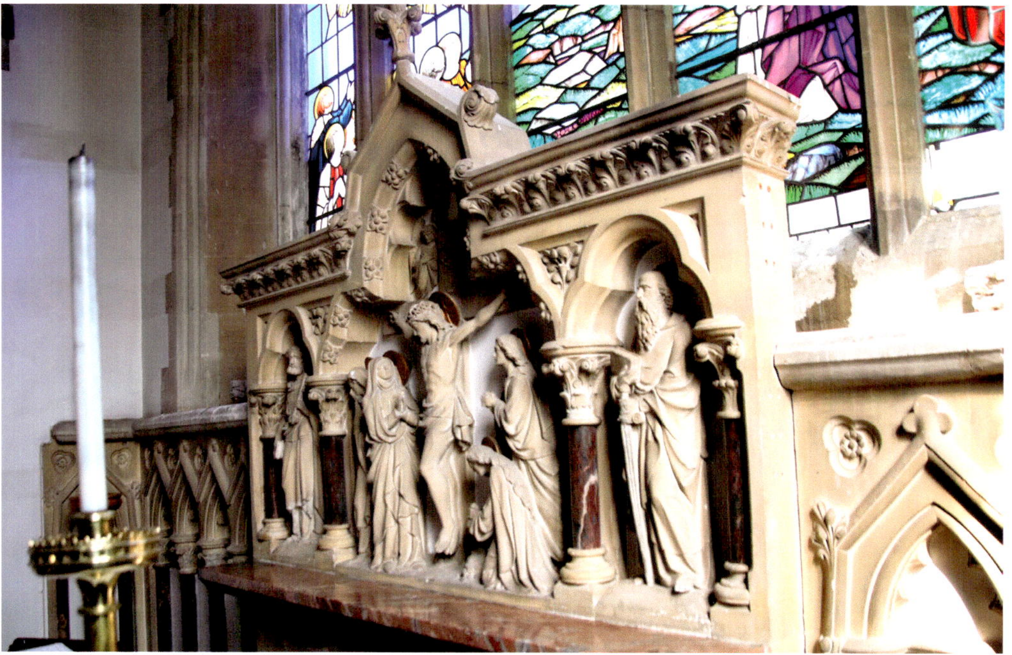

Window, Clifton Church.

Reredos, Clifton Church.

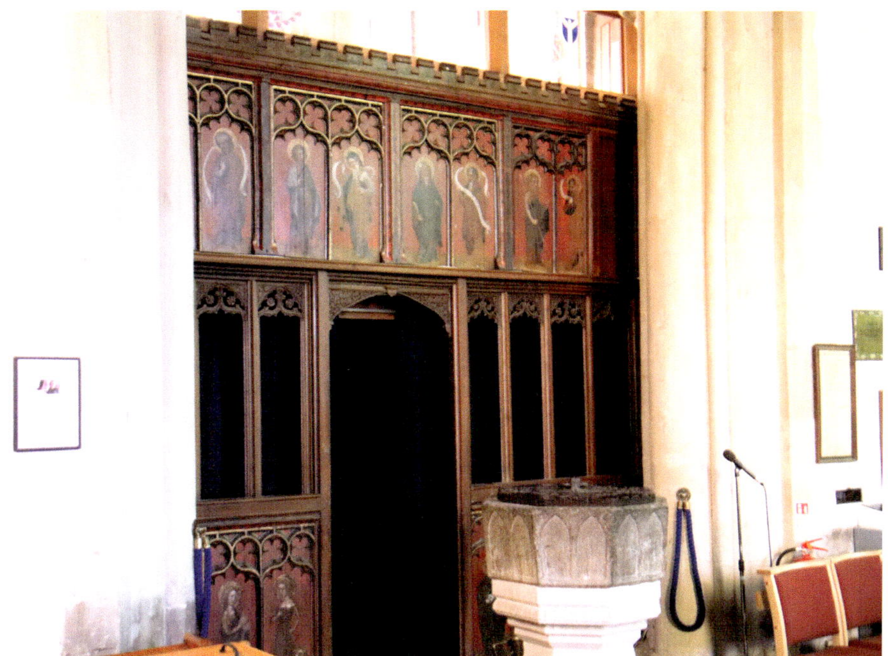

Screen and font, Clifton Church.

The church also contains two late medieval treasures. The first is the alabaster altar tomb of Sir Thomas Lucy and his wife. Sir Thomas died in 1520 and was server to King Henry VIII. The second can be found behind the font at the west end of the church at the entrance to the tower. It is known as the Clifton Screen, a medieval survivor with sixteen painted figures on it. These are of seven prophets and nine saints. It was carefully restored in 1992, revealing the figures on a brick red backdrop.

The font itself is probably the oldest object in the church and, if original, dates back to the thirteenth century. Only the bowl of the font can be considered medieval as it stands on a much more modern base.

All Saints at Clifton has been in a benefice with All Saints Church in Southill since 1994, and more recently, St Mary's Church at Haynes since September 2021.

12. CLOPHILL, ST MARY

The Central Bedfordshire village of Clophill is situated on the eastern side of the main A6 road from Luton to Bedford. The village nestles in the Flit River valley. It also has the popular Greensand Ridge Walk passing through it. The 2021 census shows a population of 1,750 living within its boundaries.

The village boasts two church buildings, of which St Mary's Old Church is no longer in use, having been replaced by a new church in the nineteenth century. The old church of St Mary the Virgin was built in the fourteenth century on a hill at the edge of the village, offering outstanding views over the northern Chiltern Hills.

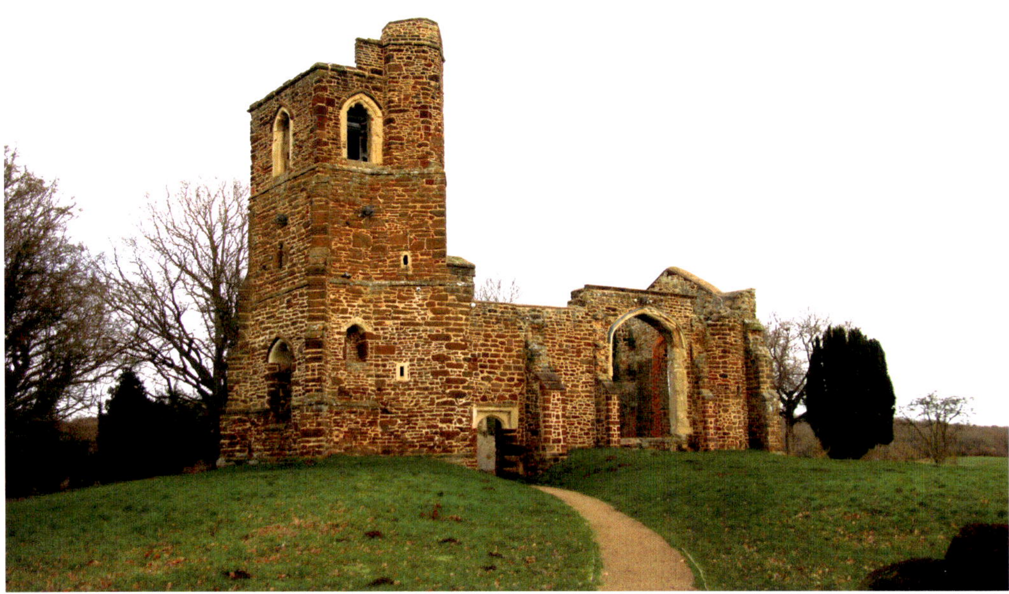

Clophill, Old St Mary's Church.

In the last 150 years, village worship has been conducted at the new church, leaving the old building to fall into disrepair. The 'old' church was used latterly as a mortuary chapel, holding bodies before burial in the adjacent cemetery. It was, however, to achieve notoriety in the 1960s following claims that the desecration of several female graves was the work of Satan worshippers, whose ceremonies were known to have a female at their centres. In short, many believe the church to be associated with dark magic, not least because the church was built the wrong way round, facing away from, rather than towards, God. These Satanic-linked actions were later to be refuted by claims that these actions had been carried out by a group of local students. Over the years, the building has suffered from continued vandalism, including the theft of the lead from the church roof in the mid-twentieth century. The ruined church site is now under the auspices of Clophill Heritage Trust. As well as offering guided tours of the observation tower, the Trust offers the use of four eco-lodges nearby.

As the village population grew, plans were drawn up to enlarge the building. In the 1840s, those plans were changed and a new Victorian church was built on the village High Street, closer to the majority of parishioners. This new St Mary's Church incorporated several items removed from the old church. These included the lychgate, two church bells, the font and numerous pieces of timber. At the same time, the chancel and the galleries were removed in order that the building could be turned from a church into a chapel.

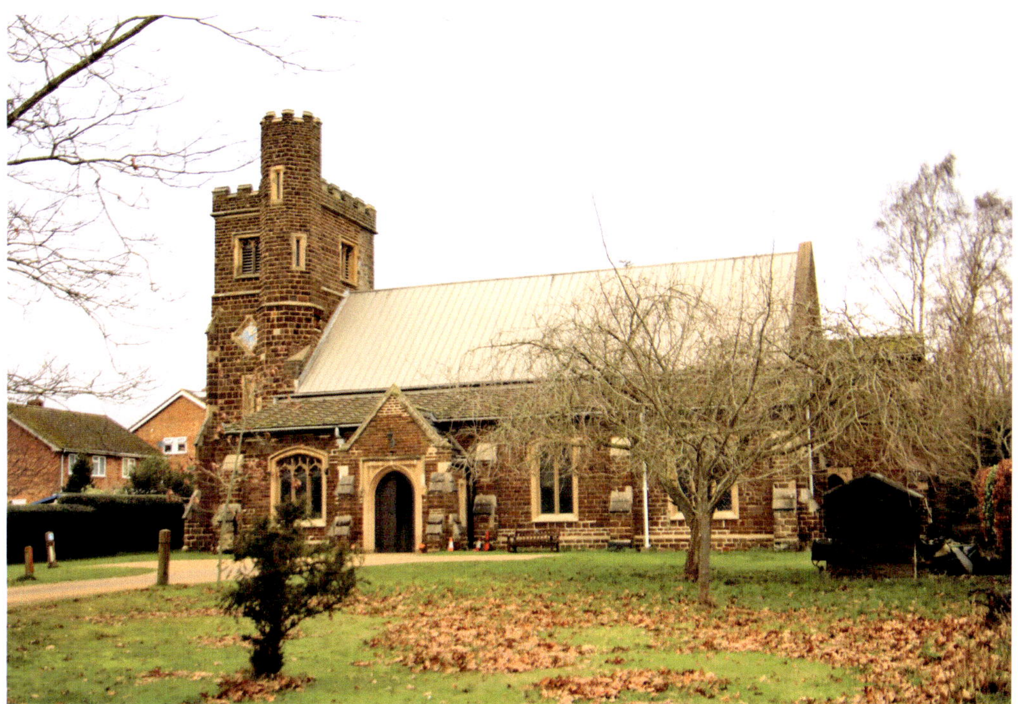

Clophill Church.

Sadly, dry rot was detected in the new church's roof in the mid-1960s, leading to its replacement by the pitched roof that remains in use today. This new church is part of the benefice of Clophill and Maunden and prides itself on being at the very centre of village community life.

13. Cranfield, St Peter and St Paul

Cranfield is situated between Bedford and Milton Keynes in the west of Bedfordshire. Once a quiet, rural village, it now has a bustling university and airfield. Its population is just over 7,000.

St Peter and St Paul's Church is situated near the centre of the old village. One enters the church grounds via a lychgate which dates back to the mid-nineteenth century. The early English church seen today was constructed of coarse limestone towards the end of the twelfth century. The middle of the thirteenth century saw the church extended. This was due to its rise in popularity as a rumour circulated that it had a holy spring which helped treat eye infections. It was never proven.

The embattled tower originally had a lead spire. This fell into decay and was replaced by a weathervane in 1975. On entering the church through the south porch, a list of rectors dating back to 1113, including the period of the Black Death, is visible.

The church has a splendid interior. Just inside the door is a fifteenth-century 'stoup', reminding us of the Roman Catholic and Jewish traditions of

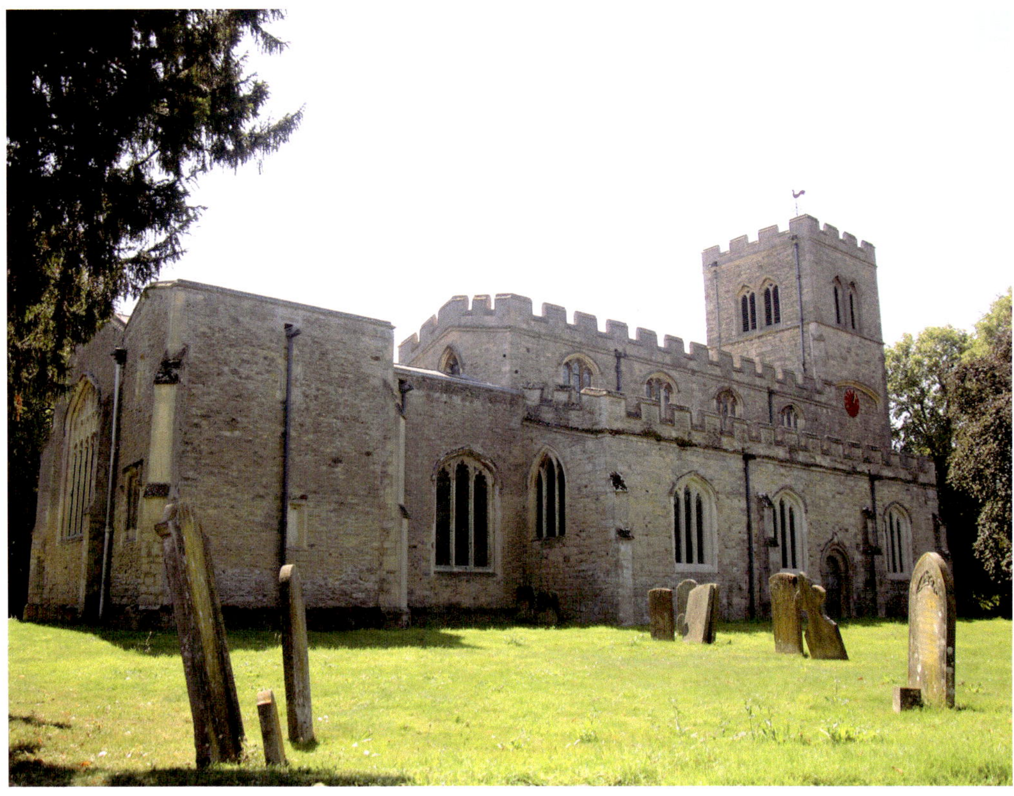

Cranfield Church.

washing on entering a place of worship. The church is, perhaps, best known for its angel roof. With so much of interest here, it would be easy to miss the fact that the church is the only one in Bedfordshire to have two fonts. The modern font, from Victorian times, is used today. The older font from the fifteenth century was found in pieces buried in the churchyard. William White from USA paid to have it repaired in 1938 in memory of an ancestor buried there in 1530 – it has its original lining and the staple was still in one of the pieces. This was used to bolt the lid closed to prevent witches from stealing the holy water.

Cranfield church is in a benefice with St Nicholas at Hulcote with St Mary the Virgin at Salford.

14. Dunstable, Priory Church of St Peter

The town of Dunstable is the fourth largest in the county of Bedfordshire, with a population of around 35,000. The priory church occupies a prime location close to the A5, Watling Street, in the centre of the town, situated in the public priory gardens.

It is thought by many to be the oldest church in Bedfordshire. Had it not been for the Dissolution of the Monasteries by Henry VIII, Dunstable could

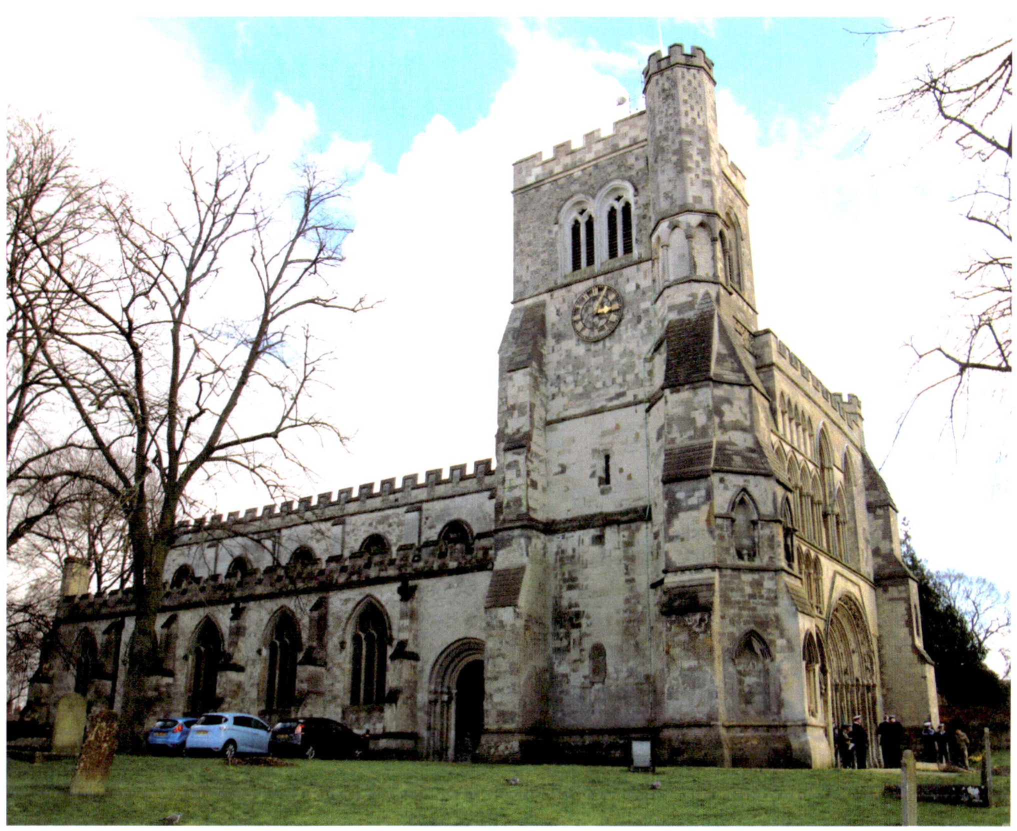

Dunstable Priory Church.

have become a city with the priory church becoming one of the great English cathedrals.

Its history is complex. It was founded in 1132 by Henry I, for Augustine canons who were evicted at the time of Dissolution. Parts of the priory church have, however, survived as part of St Peter's parish church today.

The church's connection with Henry VIII was cemented in history in 1533. On 10 May that year, the court which presided over Henry VIII's annulled marriage to Catherine of Aragon, who was living at nearby Ampthill at the time, was held in the Lady Chapel of the priory church. Archbishop Thomas Cranmer annulled the king's marriage leaving him to marry Anne Boleyn. This was the beginning of the break from Rome and the Pope's authority had been publicly flaunted. This was an essential turning point for the creation of the Anglican Church. The Lady Chapel was demolished after the priory was dissolved in 1540.

Entering the church, the eye is drawn to the magnificent screen, with its five open bays. By contrast, above the altar are two modern windows which illuminate the centrepiece below, a set of three gilded statues below a canopy. A truly beautiful building both inside and out.

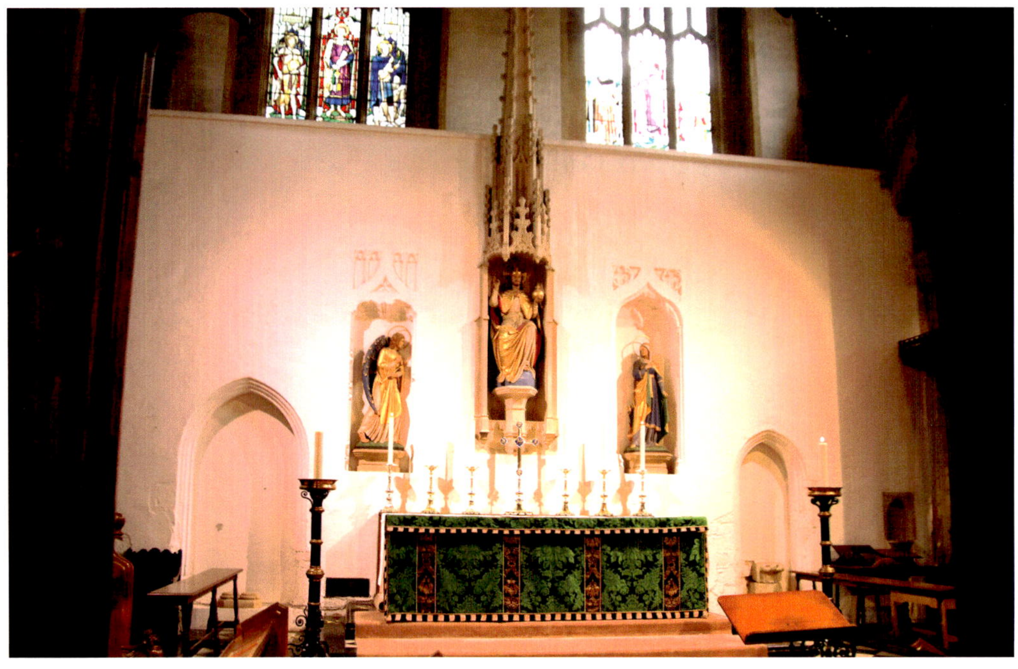

Inside Dunstable Priory Church.

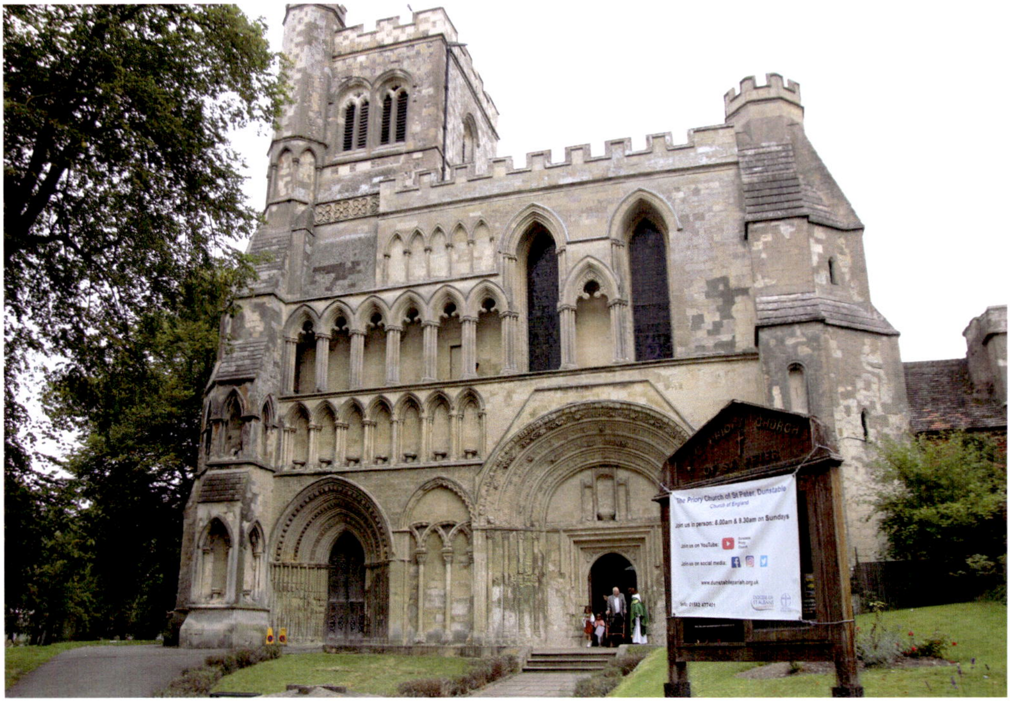

Dunstable Priory Church.

15. EATON BRAY, ST MARY

Eaton Bray lies 3 miles to the southwest of the town of Dunstable, with a local population of around 2,500.

St Mary's Church lies in the centre of the village, just off the main High Street, becoming a listed building in February 1967. It serves the recently created benefice of Eaton Bray with Edlesborough. The parish has been enlarged to include these two villages together with Dagnall and Northall as well as the settlement of Wellhead.

The general impression created from the outside view is of a fifteenth-century church, however, there are many features inside dating to the thirteenth century, demonstrating that St Mary's has been a place of prayer for 800 years. On entering the church, it soon becomes obvious that the two lines of arches are very different. The south being an example of early thirteenth-century craftsmanship, its octagonal pillars are carved at the top with leaf ornaments. By contrast, the north arches are very ornate with complex pillars each having eight shafts and intricate leaf designs at the pier top.

During the nineteenth century the church fell into decay and dilapidation, with even anecdotal accounts of falling masonry during worship. The Revd John Hall Doe, the vicar from 1870 to 1890, started a restoration fund. This initiative showed his good intentions despite having a reputation for being an angry, stubborn man, disliked by many. He sought the advice of an architect and subsequently organised the shoring up of the northern aisle. With the support of his wife and daughters, Doe led the fundraising through musical concerts which made a considerable contribution to both village life and the church restoration fund. This was at a time when the village was particularly poor due to the agricultural depression.

The present roof has been completely renovated. The wall posts have interesting fifteenth-century corbels, carved with faces, which could well be those of local

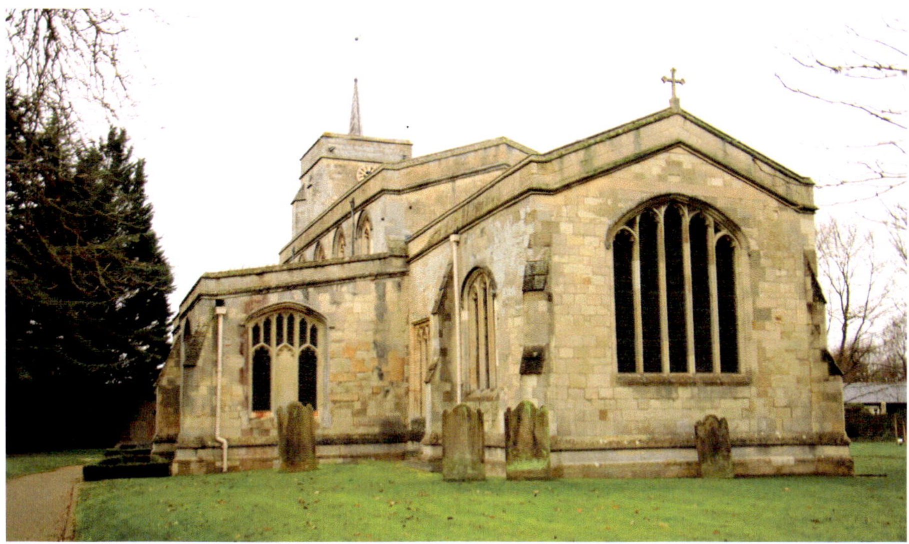

Eaton Bray Church.

villagers at the time. A particular example is the 'green man' above the pulpit which takes the form of a fertility symbol, complete with foliage growing out of his mouth. Many believe this demonstrates the link between pagan ideas and the Christian faith of the time.

Today's splendid organ was built in the late 1980s, after £55,000 had been raised. The then organist of St Paul's Cathedral drew up the specifications enabling a local Hertfordshire artisan to build it.

The pair of fire-hooks hanging either side of this organ were originally placed in the church to enable any villagers to use in the event of fire, so they could drag any burning thatch from the roofs of local homes. Other examples of the many intriguing tales regarding the church and its history are found in a booklet promoted within the church.

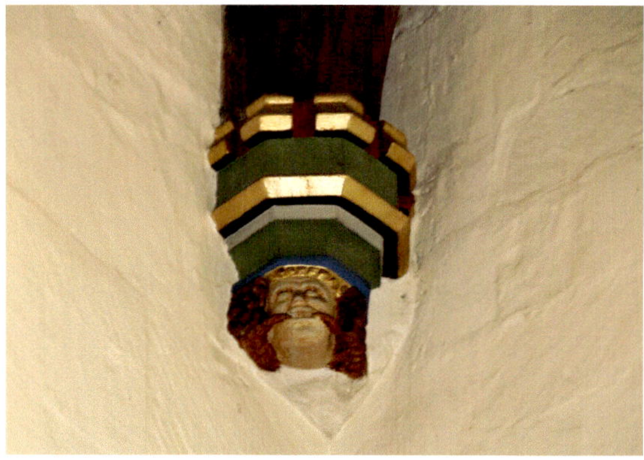

Left: Corbels, Eaton Bray.

Below: Fire hooks and organ, Eaton Bray.

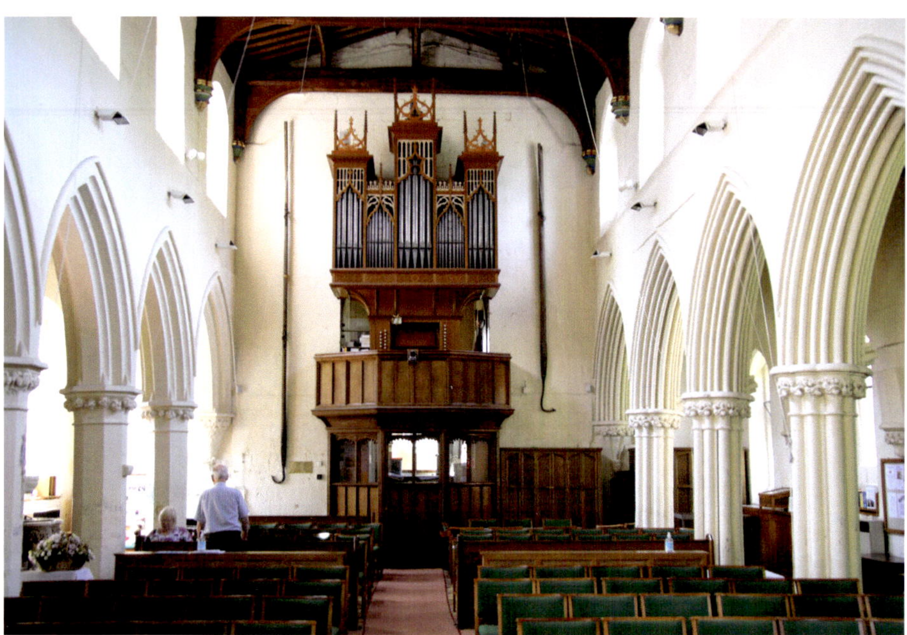

16. Elstow, St Mary and St Helena

The village of Elstow lies a couple of miles to the south of Bedford town centre and is now somewhat engulfed by Bedford's urban development.

There are no other villages in the county of Bedfordshire that can namedrop on the scale of Elstow, with William the Conqueror, Henry VIII and John Bunyan all having links with the parish.

Elstow Abbey was founded in the eleventh century by Judith, Countess of Huntingdon, who was a niece of William the Conqueror, classing it as a royal foundation. By the time of its closure, it was home to twenty-three Benedictine nuns, together with the abbess. Its demise came about when it surrendered to Henry VIII at the time of the Dissolution of the Monasteries in the 1530s.

The church was originally dedicated to St Mary and the Holy Trinity. Later, a chapel was built which was dedicated to St Helena, mother of the first Christian Roman Emperor, Constantine the Great – hence the church's name today. Another relic of the monastery's days is a small, vaulted building adjoined to the south side of the church. This was originally a parlour, believed for the abbess, and today finds use as the vestry.

Elstow also has a claim to fame as the baptism site of the famous writer and preacher John Bunyan, who was born here in 1628. It is said that not only was he baptised here using the present perpendicular font but was also known to ring the church bells. The nearby village green was one of Bunyan's childhood haunts and remains home to the Moot Hall, which is now a museum.

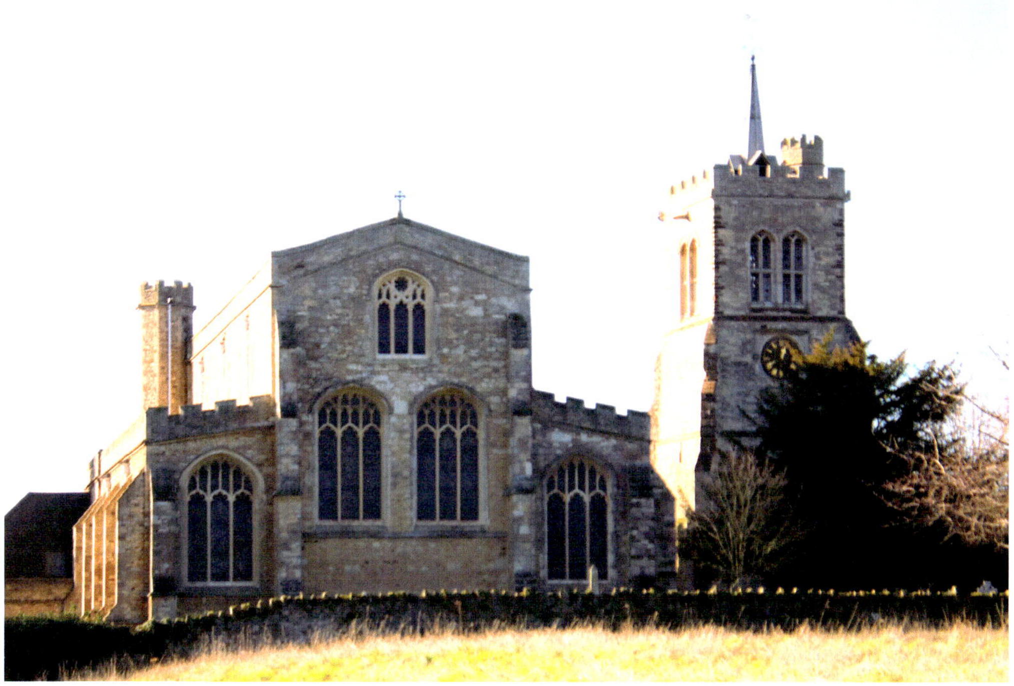

Elstow Church.

Today, the church is accessed from Elstow High Street, via Church End and, in its present dimensions, has served as the parish church since the days of Elizabeth I. Its tower stands separately to the northwest of the church and dates from the fourteenth century.

On entering the church, the six magnificent arches serve as a reminder that the church has been a place of worship since Norman times. There are a significant number of artefacts to be found within the building today. Scholars of Bunyan believe that a small, blocked door at the west end of the north aisle was the inspiration for his 'Wicked Gate' in the *Pilgrim's Progress* through which Christians would pass for deliverance. The church also contains many brasses and tombs, with the fifteenth-century brasses, in particular, being popular with brass enthusiasts. These brasses include two depicting abbess Elizabeth Hervey and her grandmother, Dame Margery.

Elstow church forms a benefice with St Michael's and All Angels, Bedford; St Mary the Virgin, Cardington; All Saints, Houghton Conquest; and All Saints, Wilstead.

17. Eyeworth, All Saints

Eyeworth, sometimes known as Eyworth, is a very small rural village with a population of ninety. It is situated 4 miles east of Biggleswade and is 12 miles southeast of Bedford. The parish's eastern boundary borders Cambridgeshire and Hertfordshire at the River Rhee.

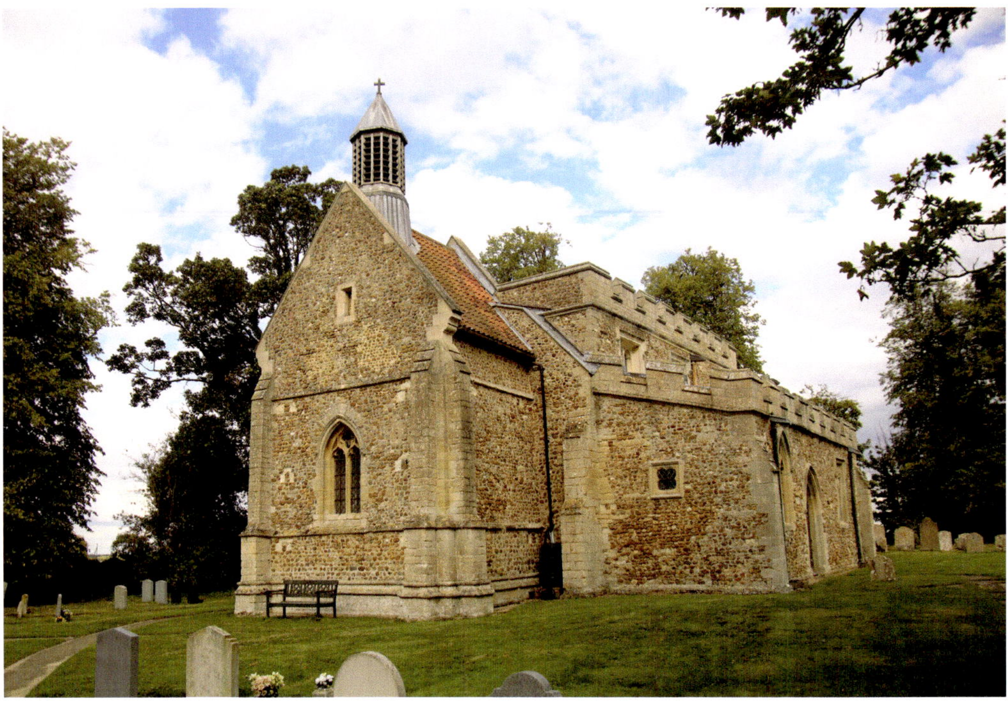

Eyeworth Church.

The church, All Saints, is set at the end of a track, a field length away from the High Street which goes from Biggleswade to Wrestlingworth. The fabrication of the church is mainly ironstone cobbles and other field stones with a limestone dressing. Other materials, however, have been used through the ages for renovations and repairs.

The tower was originally built in the fourteenth century with an imposing spire. A lighting strike on 20 September 1967 destroyed it and this was replaced, in 1970, by a modern bell turret and tiled roof. This gives the quaint old, embattled church a very unusual ancient and modern look.

Once inside, one's eyes are drawn to the pride of the church, a splendid marble altar tomb of Sir Edmund Anderson (1530–1605). He was Chief Justice under Elizabeth I but better known as a judge at the trial of Mary, Queen of Scots and Sir Walter Raleigh. Historical rumour has it that he was a witch hunter and claimed to have executed more than thirty witches, both male and female. The rumours also include that, due to Satan's powers, he thought the outcomes of trials should be decided on presumption and that no indisputable proof was necessary. A frightening thought in today's world of justice.

The chancel also has a monument to his son, Sir Francis, and both of his wives. A third monument in the southwest chancel is to Edmund Anderson (1607–38), son of Sir Francis.

All Saints Church is in a benefice with St Mary Magdalen, at Dunton, and St Peter's at Wrestlingworth.

18. FELMERSHAM, ST MARY

The church of St Mary's, in the village of Felmersham, dates back to 1220, around the same time as Salisbury Cathedral. The original church was completed around 1240 and remains largely unchanged to this day, apart from a few minor modifications in the fourteenth and fifteenth centuries. It became a Grade I listed building in the 1960s.

Approaching the village from nearby Radwell, the seven-arch bridge across the River Great Ouse offers spectacular views of this, one of the finest churches in the county. It sits on a hill high above the river, providing a stunning focal point for Felmersham and its surrounds. The village lies in the northeast corner of the county, with a population of around 800.

The original east window, in memory of Thomas Abbot Green who died in 1855, was damaged during the Second World War. Its replacement has a poignant local family story to tell. The Wells family, from nearby Felmersham Grange, commissioned artist Francis Spear in 1951 to design a window in memory of their three sons and their nurse. The three men gave their lives in the Second World War. Each son was a member of one of the three armed services. The magnificent window, therefore, reflects the risen Christ with St Mary and St Christopher to his right, and St Thomas and St James to his left. These represent the name of their nurse and the three sons. The three services' dedicated saints are also depicted within the window.

The Wells family also donated three additional bells in loving memory of their sons. This increased the total number of church bells to eight, necessitating strengthening of the tower to take this extra weight.

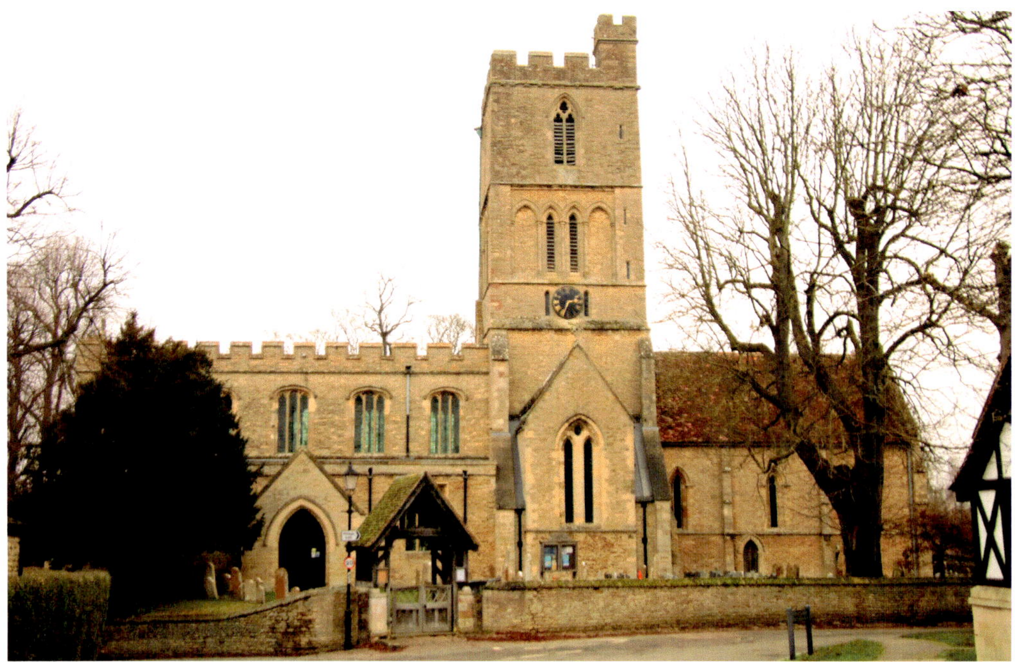

Felmersham Church.

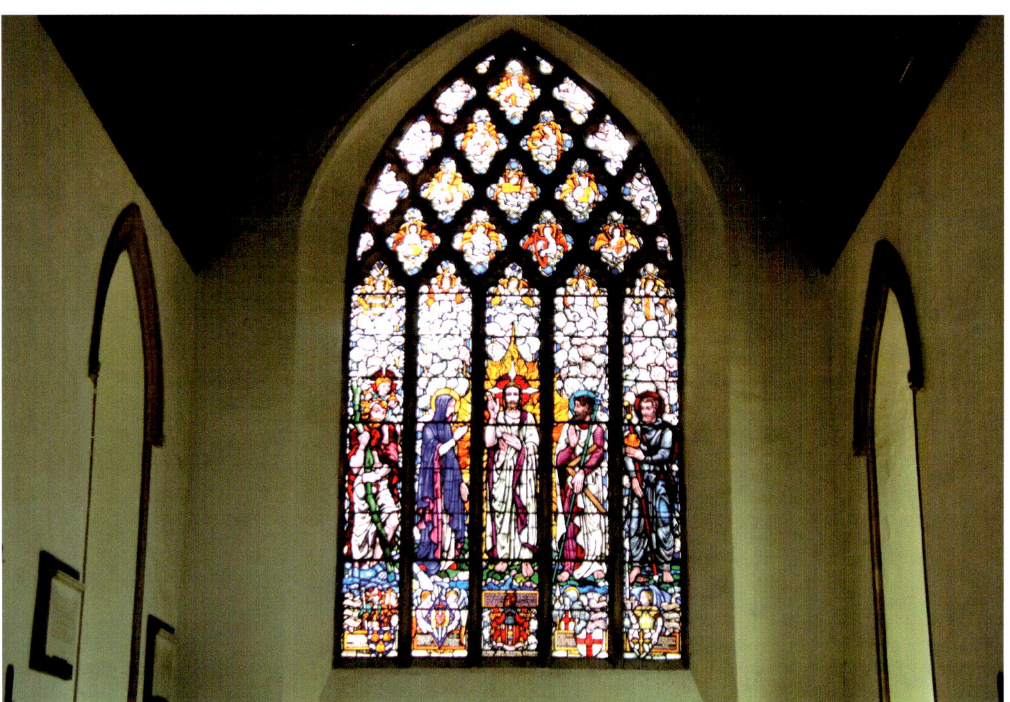

Memorial window, Felmersham.

The local parishioners are also rightly proud of their new Millennium window which replaced the previous one in the Memorial Chapel and was installed in June 2001. This modern window depicts the transfiguration of Christ, represented by a shining star on a cross as its focal point. In common with much modern works of art, the window's meaning is for each individual to interpret. The Incarnation is symbolised as a ray of light at the centre, with rays in the form of a cross extending across its whole.

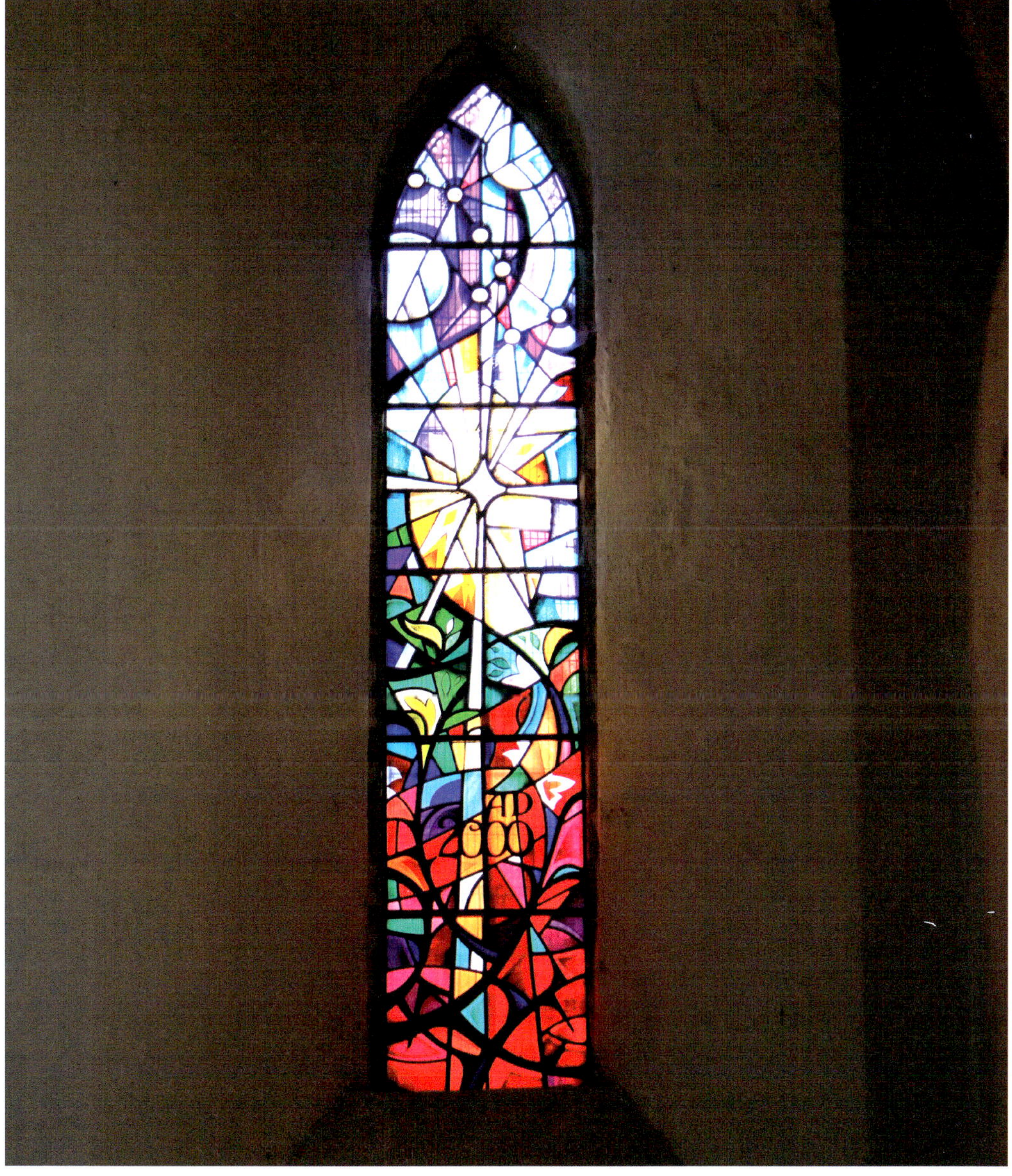

Millennium window, Felmersham.

19. Flitwick, St Peter and St Paul with St Andrew

Flitwick is mentioned in the Domesday Book as 'a hamlet on the river Flitt'. It is now a town of almost 14,000 according to the 2021 census and is situated around 10 miles from both Bedford and Luton. The church of St Peter and St Paul is on the southern edge of Flitwick in a quiet cul-de-sac.

It is thought that it started its life as a small wooden building. This was replaced by a stone building around the time of the 1086 Domesday Book. This small Norman church was, like many churches, rebuilt and extended many times. At the end of the fourteenth century a tower was added.

A lot of effort has been made to preserve the history of the architecture. In 1835, it was decided to build a north aisle extension. The Norman doorway, dating back to the twelfth century, was removed piece by piece and a detailed plan made. It was then placed in the new north aisle wall exactly how it had been originally. The etching made of the original north door hangs on the north wall inside the church.

On entering the church there is evidence of its journey through time. The circular fluted bowl of the font is from the twelfth century; however the shaft and stand are much more modern. Local myth tells us that it was thought that evil spirits lived in church fonts and therefore some had lids which were kept locked. Many people felt that this kept the spirits locked in, however it was more likely to keep the evil out of the holy water. The lid of the font in St Peter and

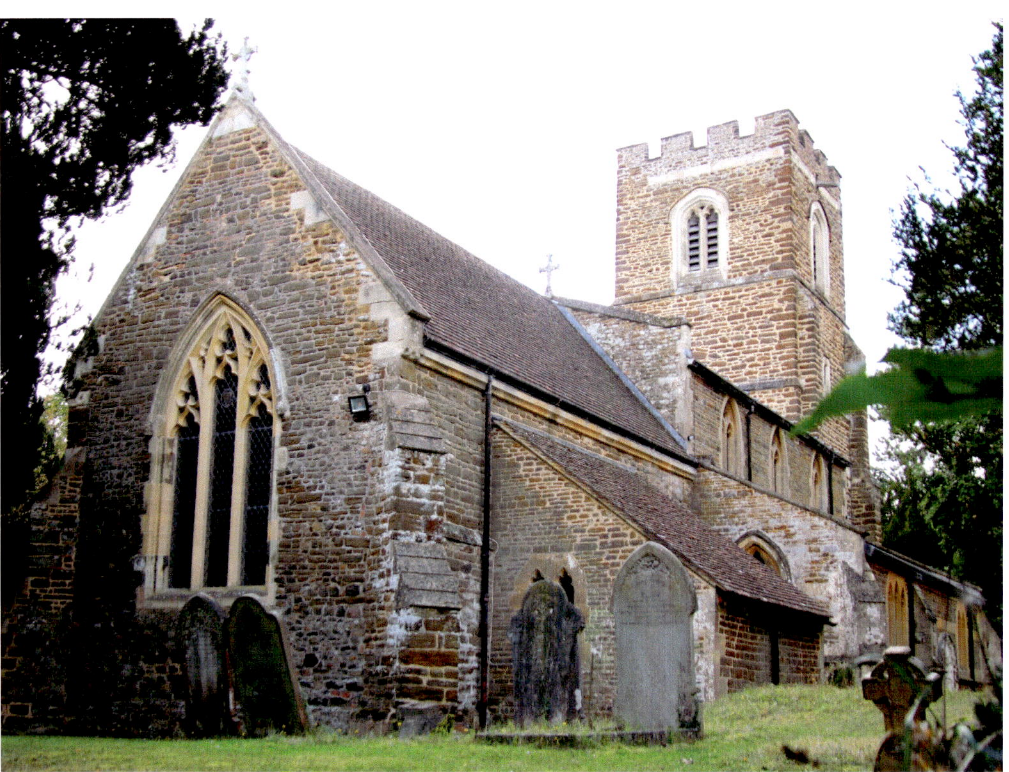

Flitwick Church.

St Paul's Church was very securely fastened for many years and was only opened and restored in the mid-nineteenth century. Over the years when the font's lid was fastened, a small basin was used as an alternative for purposes of baptism.

As one moves around the church, two modern mosaics catch the eye. These are on either side of the altar and depict Christ as the Light of The World and the Good Shepherd.

St Peter and St Paul's was in a benefice with St Andrew's, to the north of Flitwick. St Andrew's was closed in 2018, due to its dilapidated condition. The parish church is now known as St Peter and St Paul with St Andrew.

20. Great Barford, All Saints

Great Barford is a Bedfordshire village 5 miles northeast of Bedford. The village is bypassed by the A421 ring road linking Milton Keynes, Bedford and the A1. The village sits on the River Great Ouse and is home to an ancient fifteenth-century bridge. In recent times, the area beside the bridge, opposite the pub, has been a hive of activity for fishing, canoeing, paddleboarding, picnicking and sunbathing, earning it the nickname of 'Great Barford beach' – this is even though there is no beach! The grey, pinnacle tower of All Saints Church, with its four grotesque gargoyles and its little lead spire, dwarfs this area.

All Saints Church has often been referred to as 'simple in its elegance'; it is certainly finely proportioned. Most of the church is built of brown cobbles, though the tower is of limestone. The tower was built in the fifteenth century and

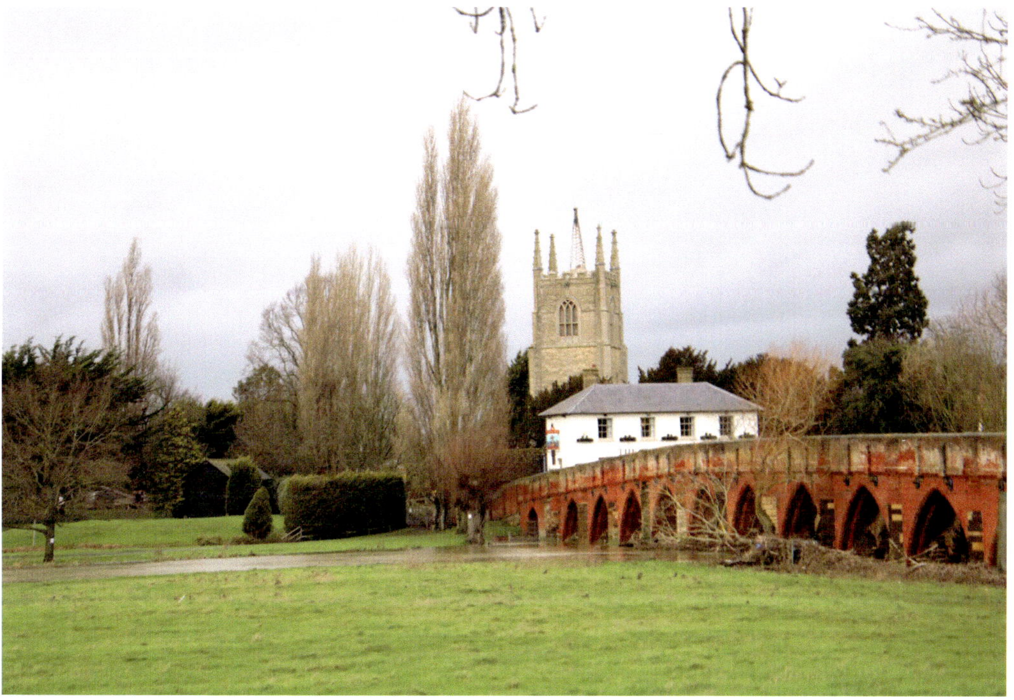

Great Barford Church.

the nave and chancel in the late fifteenth and early sixteenth centuries. Much of the church was rebuilt and added to in the nineteenth century. There is, however, some evidence left of what is thought to be the original Anglo-Saxon building. At the end of the nave, on the outside, the short and wide, and long and narrow stonework was a feature of pre-1066 architecture.

On entering the church, one notices that the font, standing in the south aisle, is a genuine medieval feature dating back to the thirteenth century. It was probably retained from the original medieval church and reinstated after the nineteenth-century rebuild. The rebuilding was sympathetically done and has, over time, included a kitchen, toilet and disabled access.

The outside of the church is compact with a neat graveyard surrounded heavily by trees. This stops the new, expanding housing estates from impacting on its tranquillity.

The church is part of the Riversmeet benefice, with Blunham, Roxton, Tempsford and Little Barford.

21. HARLINGTON, ST MARY

Located 5 miles south of the market town of Ampthill, the large village of Harlington sits around a mile to the east of the Ampthill to Dunstable A5120 road. It is bordered to the west by the Bedford to London railway line and also the M1 which is around a mile west of the village. Today, the village has a population of approximately 2,300.

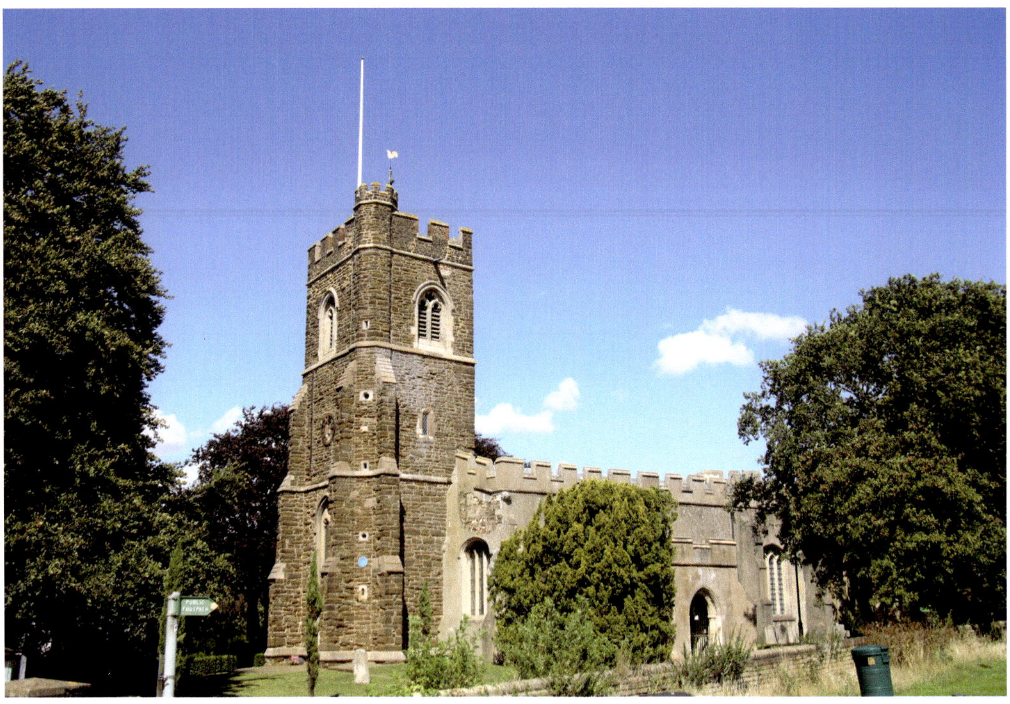

Harlington Church.

Harlington is situated on a ridge of boulder clay, sloping down in all directions from St Mary's Church, which stands 360 feet above sea level. Situated in the middle of the village, the church offers wide views across the south of the county of Bedfordshire.

Part of the church dates from the twelfth century and, like many churches, there was probably a place of worship there by 1086, as the Domesday Book mentions a priest at Harlington. The church was rebuilt, broadly in its present form, in the fourteenth century. The tower, which was added in the fifteenth century, is faced with Northamptonshire ironstone, whereas the remainder of the church together with its interior is of local Totternhoe clunch.

The church has a plain south porch, above which is a sundial dating back to at least 1686. St Mary's was restored in the Victorian era and more changes were made in the twentieth century. In 1929, a glass window featuring John Bunyan was installed. Later, an altar table was made from the oak tree under which John Bunyan had preached. This table was placed in the chancel.

Outside, on the stair turret, there is a blue plaque commemorating the first English National Steeplechase. This was 4.5 miles and went from the church

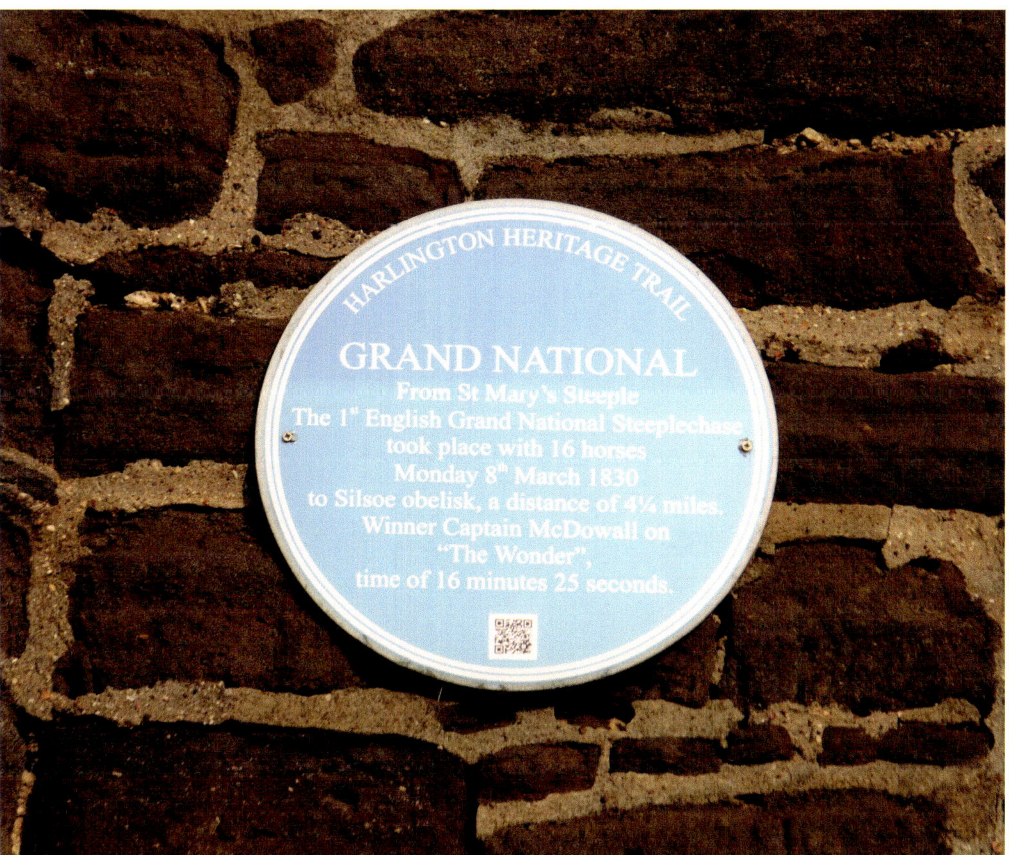

Blue plaque, Harlington.

tower finishing at the obelisk in Wrest Park. This momentous event took place in March 1830.

St Mary the Virgin, Harlington, forms a benefice with St Nicholas' in Tingrith and St Mary Magdalene in Westoning.

22. HOUGHTON REGIS, ALL SAINTS

The town of Houghton Regis was once just a small village. It is bordered by the Chiltern Hills and situated 1 mile north of Dunstable, 5 miles west of Luton, close to the Buckinghamshire border. Its character changed when it became a 'London overspill' town in the 1950s and '60s. Its population today is approximately 25,000.

All Saints Church is situated in the old village centre, on the A5120 which links the A5 to the M1. The church was built in the fourteenth century, although an earlier Saxon church dating from AD 1086 is mentioned in the Domesday Book and likely to be on the site of the present church.

Most of the present building dates from the fourteenth century, with the tower and the nave's roof and ceiling being rebuilt in the fifteenth. All Saints Church is often described as being in Rectilinear Gothic style. This style developed in northern France and was popularised in England in the fourteenth and fifteenth centuries. It was characterised by its vertical lines, perpendicular tracery and intricate stonework.

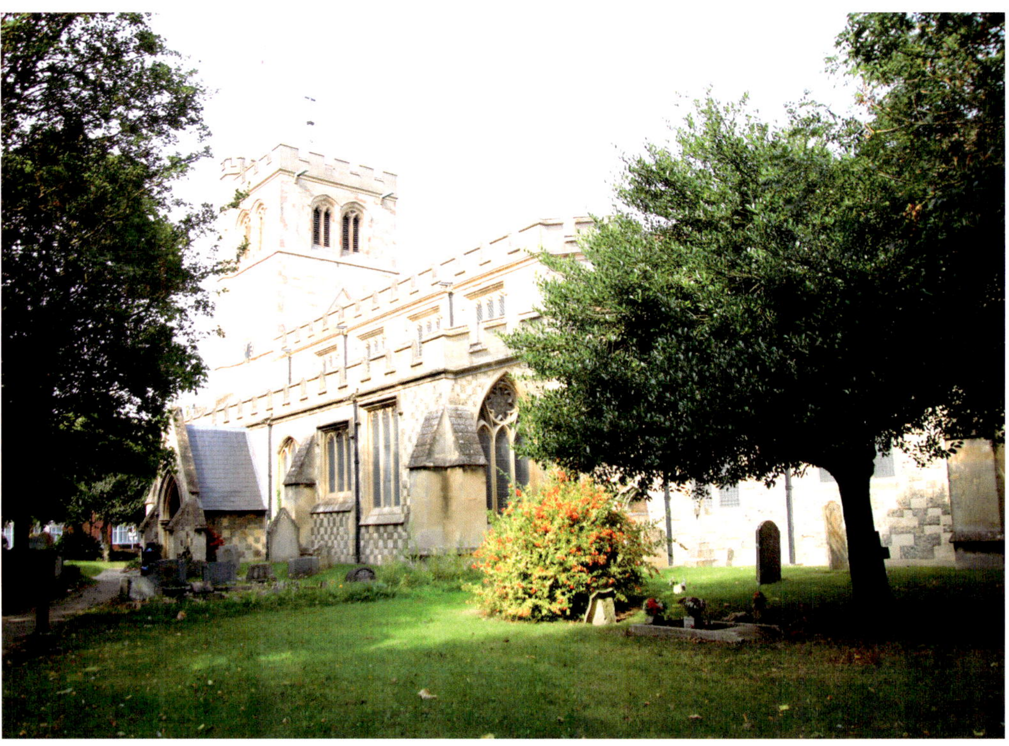

Houghton Regis Church.

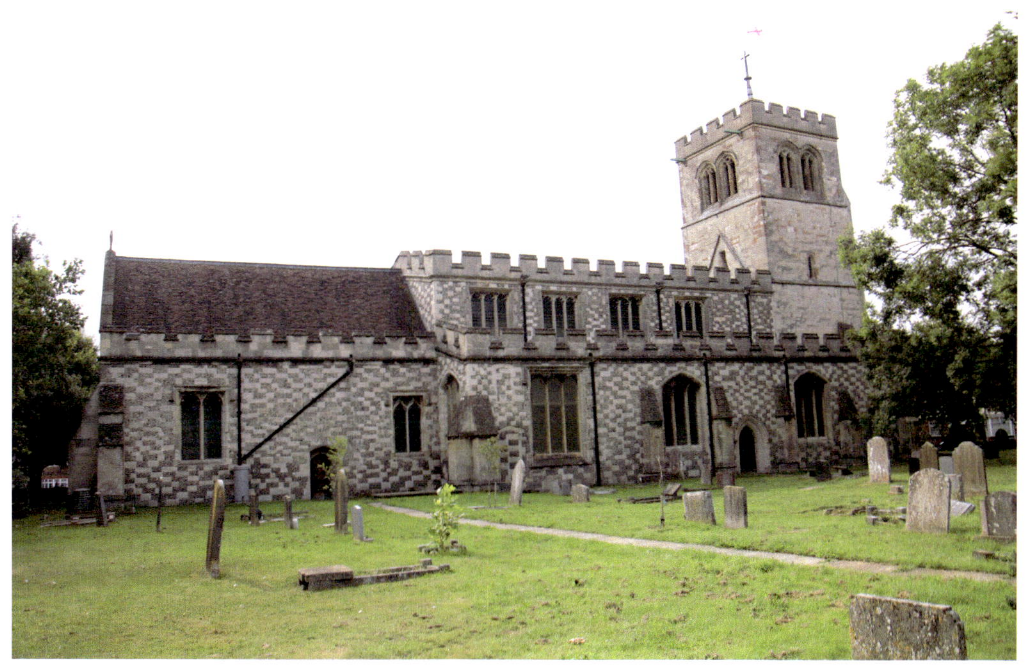

Houghton Regis Church.

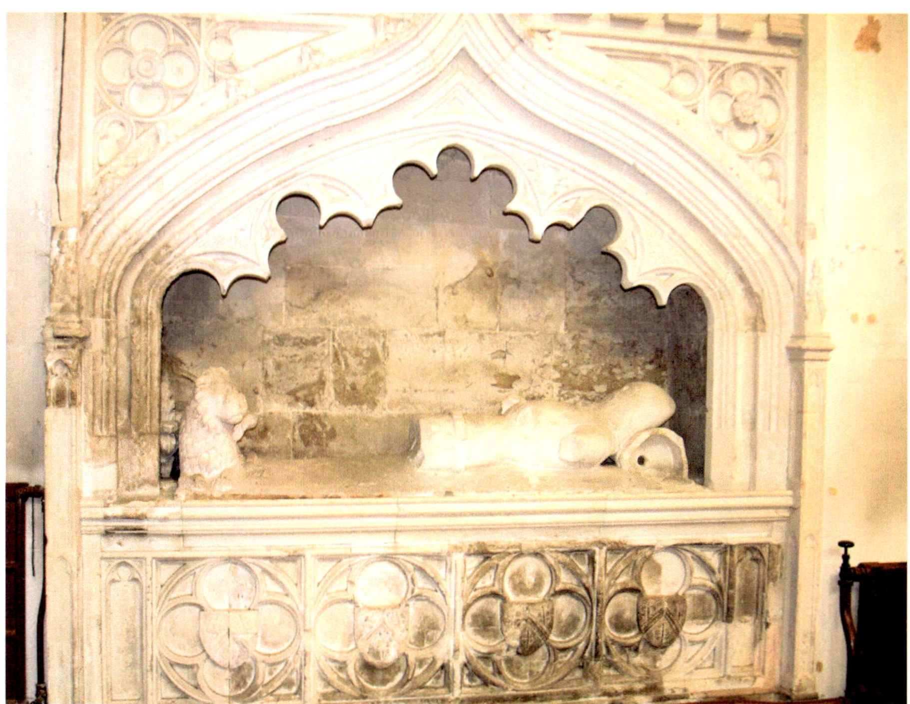

Sir John Sewell tomb, Houghton Regis.

The church is built of flint and Totternhoe stone. The latter is often called clunch and is a relatively hard chalk from the surrounding Chiltern Hills.

The external building has the chequer work so often seen in this area. The nave and aisles as well as the tower are all embattled, which gives it a stunning multi-layer effect. Inside the church there is a large tomb, believed to belong to Sir John Sewell, a knight who accompanied King Edward II's eldest son, The Black Prince, to Aquitaine in France. Only the head and torso remain with a lion protecting what would have been the feet.

The church's Norman font pre-dates its present structure. It is made of Totternhoe stone and fonts like this usually date back to the end of the twelfth century. If a font could 'namedrop', it would inevitably mention Hollywood star Gary Cooper, who was baptised and confirmed here in 1911. This celebrity was a major movie star at the end of the silent movie era through to the end of the golden age. Those of a certain age may remember him in *Ben Hur* and *High Noon*, amongst many others films.

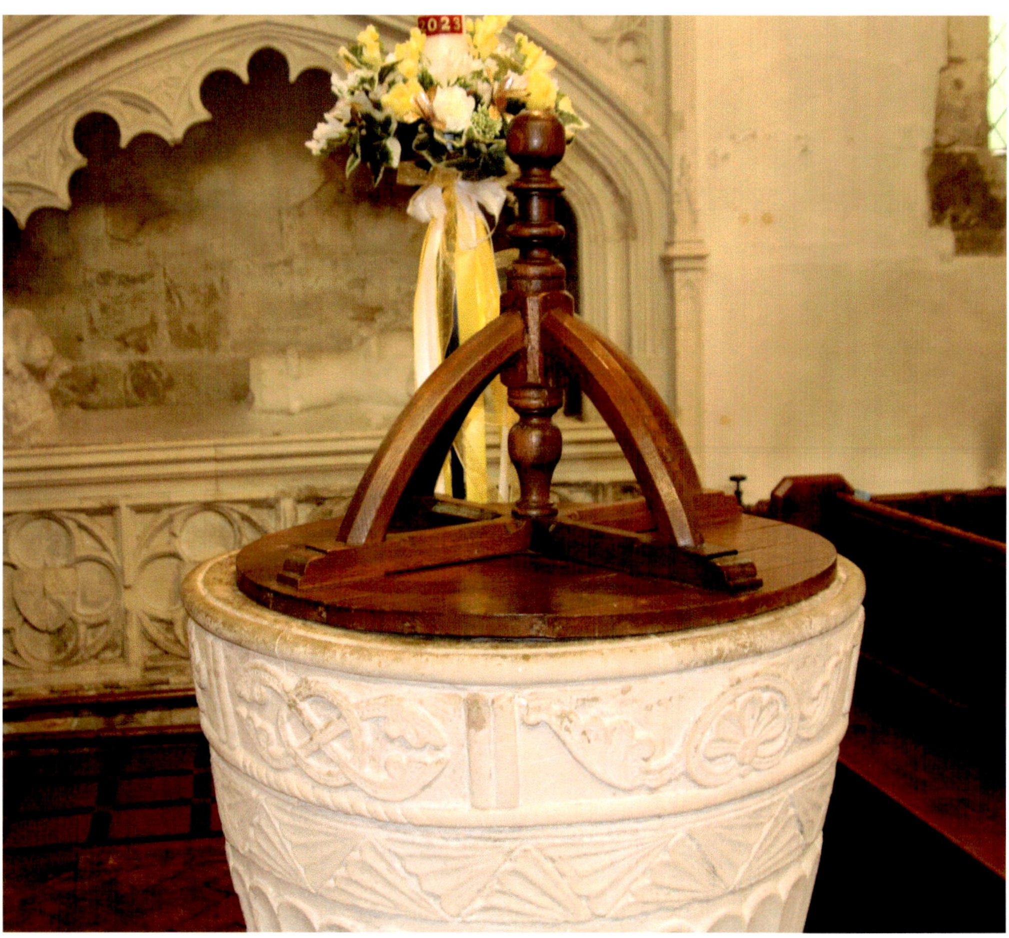

Font, Houghton Regis.

23. KEMPSTON, ALL SAINTS

Kempston is a sprawling suburb of Bedford and has a population of nearly 21,000 according to the latest census information. All Saints Church is situated some distance from the heart of Kempston in a small hamlet known as Church End. This is now in the civil parish of Kempston Rural. The hamlet has been kept quiet by the traffic being diverted along the A428 bypass. The church is close to the River Great Ouse and is to be found in what was once the original village.

All Saints was originally a small Anglo-Saxon church which has, according to local records, had a vicar since 1215. It was first altered by William the Conqueror's niece, Judith, and although altered many times since, the walls still stand today.

With the exception of the north side of the chancel, the outer walls of the church are all embattled, making it an exceptionally attractive building. The area immediately above the fifteenth-century porch originally housed a priest's room reached by an outside stone stairway. On the outside wall of the porch is a 'mass dial'. One can view a small circle of holes at regular intervals with a hole in the middle which would, at one time, have secured a pointer. This would be moved by the priest to indicate the time of the next mass. This was an early form of noticeboard or website to announce to parishioners when the next service would take place.

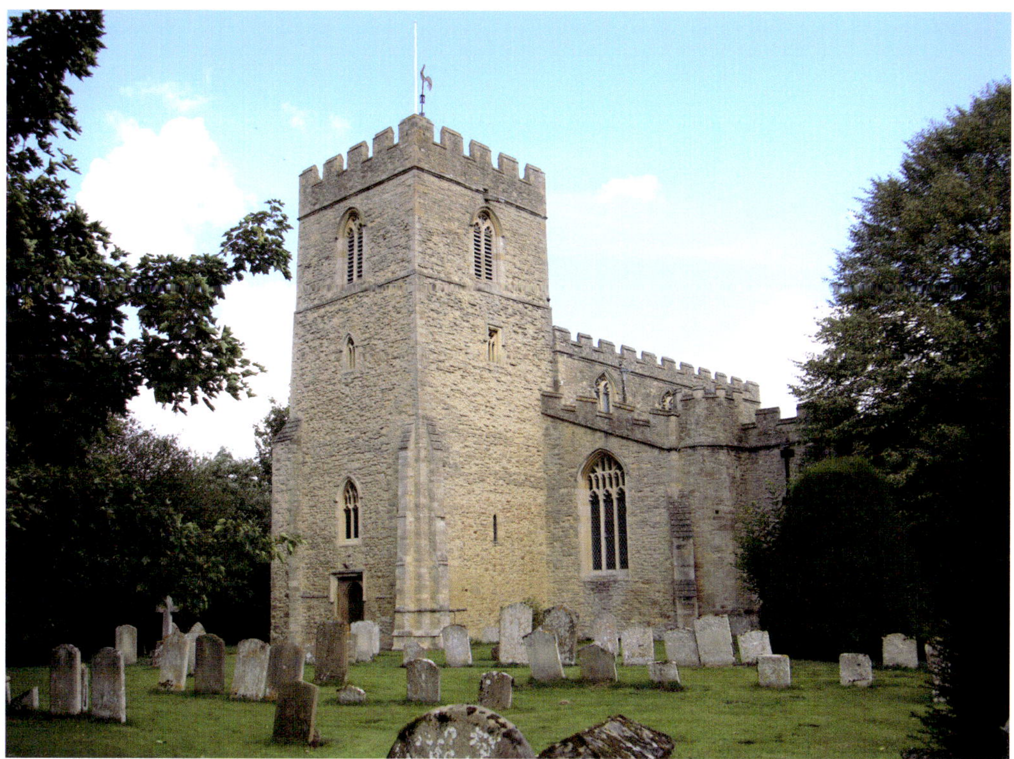

Kempston Church.

On entering the church today, one is surrounded by a distinctive piece of Norman and medieval architecture. It has a Norman arch at either end of the nave, thirteenth-century arcades and a fifteenth-century west doorway. The fourteenth-century font once had saints carved around it, but today these carvings are badly damaged. This was the result of chisel marks from when Oliver Cromwell's soldiers mutilated it. It has an ornate and distinctive oak spire cover from around the 1900s.

All Saints Church is in a benefice with St James' Church at Biddenham.

24. Langford, St Andrew

Langford, with a population of around 3,000, is a sizeable village and civil parish lying adjacent to the River Ivel a couple of miles south of Biggleswade.

The church of St Andrew's can be found in the northern part of the village, on a raised elevation on the banks of the river. The site has seen worship for almost a thousand years. It is assumed there was already a church there in 1142 when the Knights Templar commenced building their church. This was later demolished, and a new church built in the early fourteenth century, incorporating only parts of the old Templar building.

The porch and tower, unusually, stand on the south side of the building, possibly because it was the last part of the church to be built. It is also the only part of the church containing battlements. The tower is home to three bells. The treble bell dates back to 1772, the second bell to 1780, and the tenor bell was recast in 1855. These bells are housed in their original wooden frames which required treatment and repair after a death watch beetle was found in the 1970s. The wheels have

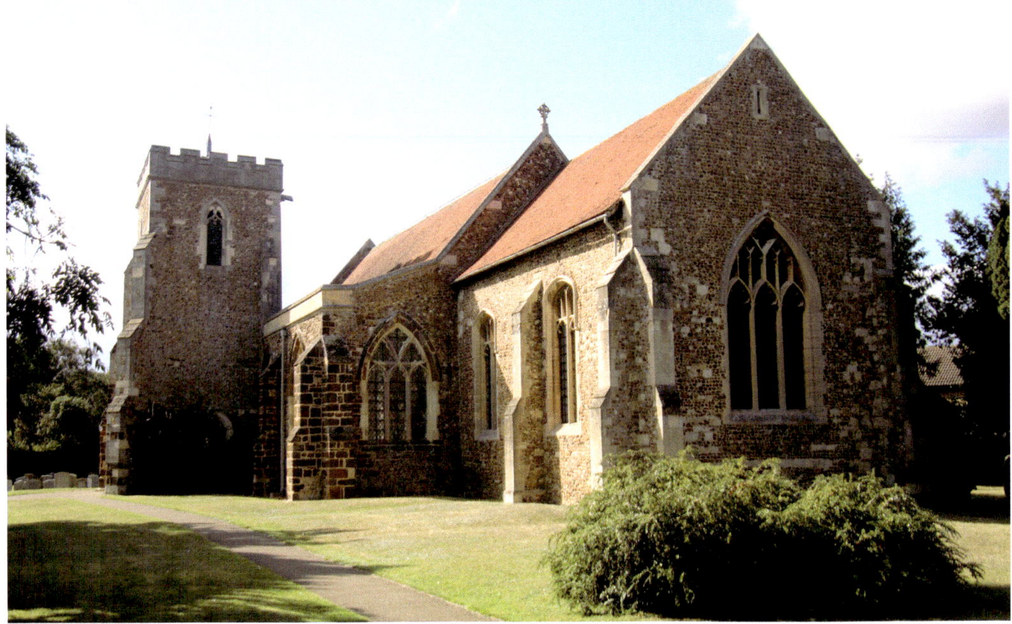

Langford Church.

been replaced by a lever mechanism enabling them to be chimed but not rung. Christmas 1980 saw them chimed in celebration of their rejuvenation.

In the church itself, the nave is made up of four bays, giving an open, spacious, airy feeling. At the top of the octagonal columns there are stone heads. It is possible to make out that most are human and one appears to be a devil with the ears of a pig!

In more recent times, worthy of mention is the vicar, Christopher Ewbank. He arrived as curate in 1867 and served the parish as vicar from 1870 to 1933, a staggering sixty-six years' service in this one parish. This surely must constitute something of a record.

On arrival in the parish, Revd Ewbank was expected to robe in the porch as there was no vestry at the time. At his insistence, as a memorial to the previous vicar, a vestry and organ chamber were erected on the north side of the church. As a memorial to Revd Ewbank himself, a screen behind the altar in the Lady Chapel was erected in 1958.

The church of St Andrew in Langford forms part of a benefice with St Mary's Church in Henlow.

25. Leighton Buzzard, All Saints

The town of Leighton Buzzard lies in the southwest of Bedfordshire, close to its border with Buckinghamshire, on the old coaching road from Oxford to Cambridge. Today, it has a population of approximately 40,000, with All Saints Church sitting, like a small cathedral, at its very heart, complete with a tower stretching up almost 200 feet.

From the moment we stepped into All Saints' churchyard we felt the sense of welcome, noting a number of people sitting reading and reflecting in the peaceful surroundings. This site has been a place of worship for almost 1,000 years, with the present church dating from 1277.

The great west door retains the original iron hinges by Thomas of Leighton. He was a famous thirteenth-century ironsmith who made the grille on the tomb of Eleanor, wife of Edward I, in Westminster Abbey.

On entering the church, the senses are arrested by the heavy air of incense. The legacy of the disastrous fire of April 1985 is of a building now splendidly blending many old artefacts with the recent restoration work.

One of the more interesting features is the church's ancient graffiti. This includes a scene where a woman is hitting a man, seemingly with a spoon. Folklore has it that these two characters were affectionally known as **Sim**on and **Nel**lie. They appear to be arguing as to whether their cake or pudding should be boiled or baked. The compromise after this argument was the creation of the first Simnel (Sim – Nel) cake. It's further believed that the graffiti dates back to the early fifteenth century, if not earlier.

The nave roof, known as the angel roof because of its magnificent carvings of angels, was donated by Alice de la Pole, Duchess of Suffolk, who was the granddaughter of the famous writer Geoffrey Chaucer. The carved angels were included in the church refurbishment and redecoration following the serious 1985 fire.

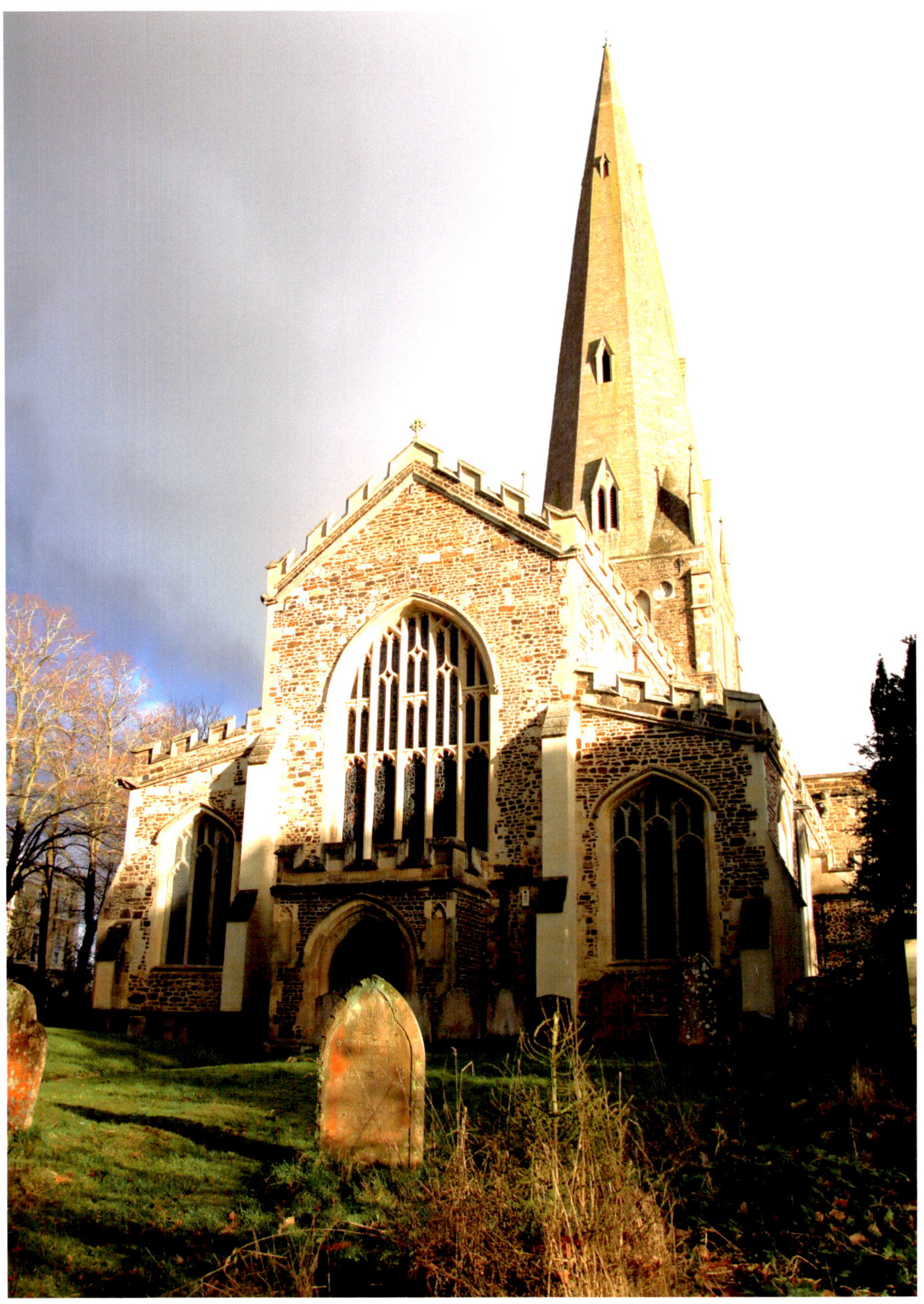

Leighton Buzzard Church.

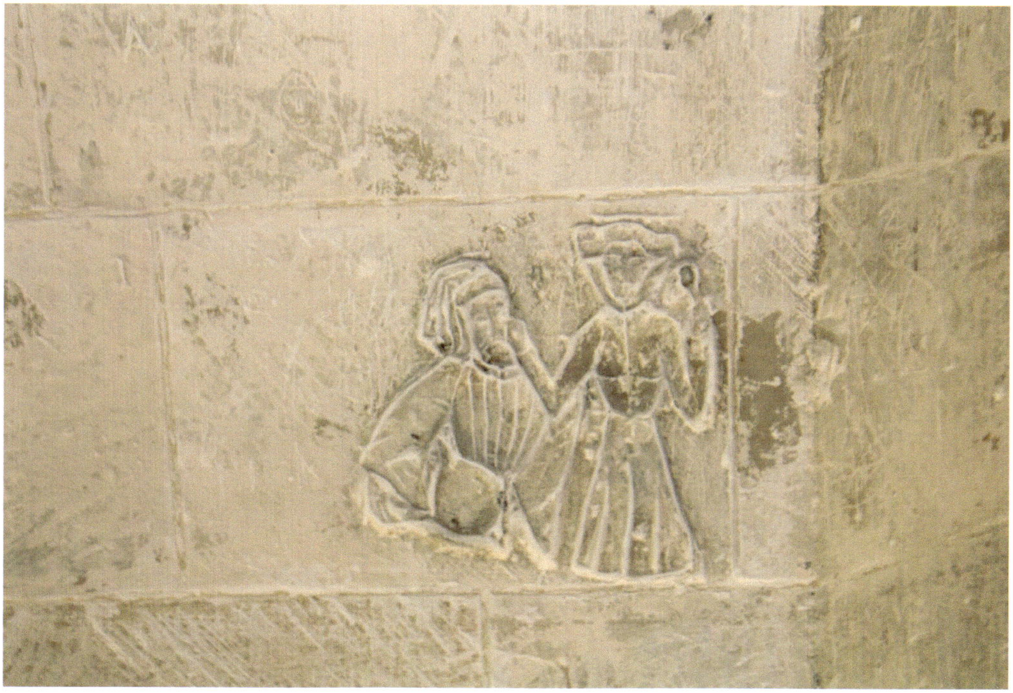

Graffiti, Leighton Buzzard.

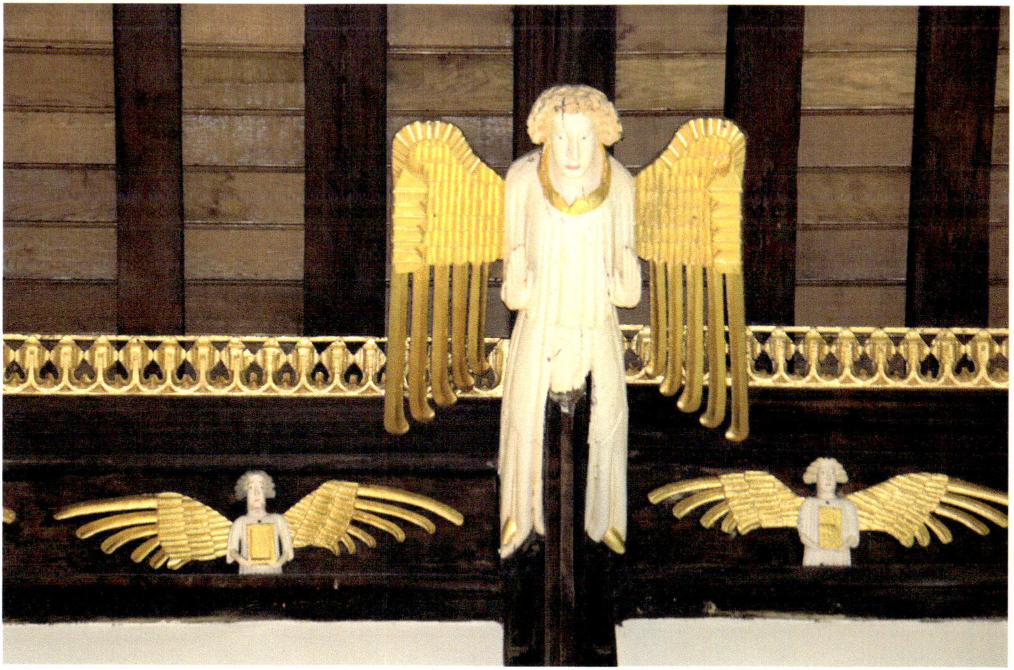

Angel roof, Leighton Buzzard.

In fact, this restoration work has been ongoing, particularly since cracks appeared in the tower and elsewhere. This restoration, both internally and externally, was in progress through to the new millennium, with work costing nearly £2 million eventually completed in 2016. This fundraising project was managed by the All Saints Preservation Trust under the guidance of Terry Warburton.

On completion of this work, Terry's efforts have been recognised by the inclusion of a new external corbel added to the east wall of the St Hugh's chapel. The figure is of Terry Warburton.

The magnificent pipe organ, with its trumpet pipes, was also rebuilt following the fire. It was later thoroughly overhauled as recently as 2018. This new organ stands on a gallery under the north arch of the central tower.

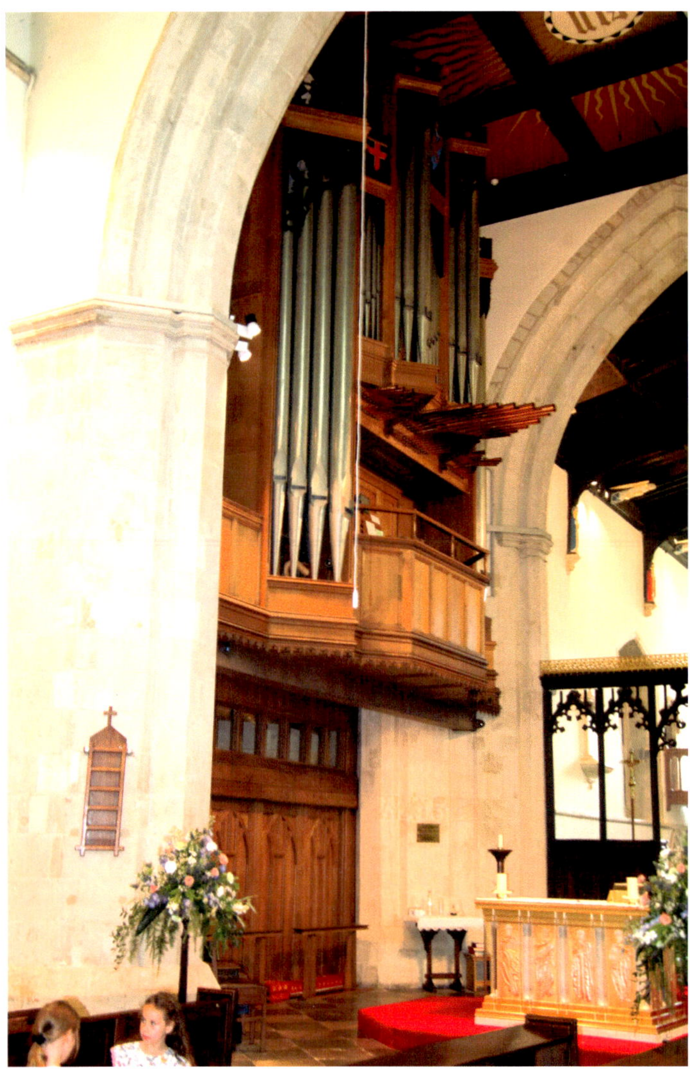

Pipe organ, Leighton Buzzard.

26. LUTON, ST MARY

The town of Luton is the county of Bedfordshire's largest, with around a third of the county's population living there. Latest figures suggest the town has a population of around 220,000. The church of St Mary's lies to the south-east of the town centre, amongst the hustle and bustle of everyday life. It is close to the town's railway station, shopping centre and university, providing an air of tranquillity both within the church and its churchyard.

With the original church having been built as early as AD 930, it has been a site of worship for more than a millennium. The current church dates from the early twelfth century and was originally a simple structure but, as the population grew, both a north and south aisle were added by the turn of the thirteenth century. This fine example of medieval architecture is one of the largest within the county.

On viewing the church's exterior one cannot help but marvel at the distinctive flint and stone, black and white chequer which covers most of the outside of the church and tower. This was restored in 1906 and this décor was continued when vestries, offices and halls were added in the 1960s.

Further back in history, rebuilding work was carried out in the fifteenth century under the supervision of Lord John Wenlock, whose family had been connected with the church since 1389. John Wenlock was known as 1st Baron Wenlock, a politician, courtier, diplomat and soldier. As a soldier he fought for both sides, the House of York and the House of Lancaster, in the War of the Roses. Many at that time fought for both houses, however his lack of ongoing allegiance to either side earned him the nickname of 'The Prince of Turncoats', often being accused of fence

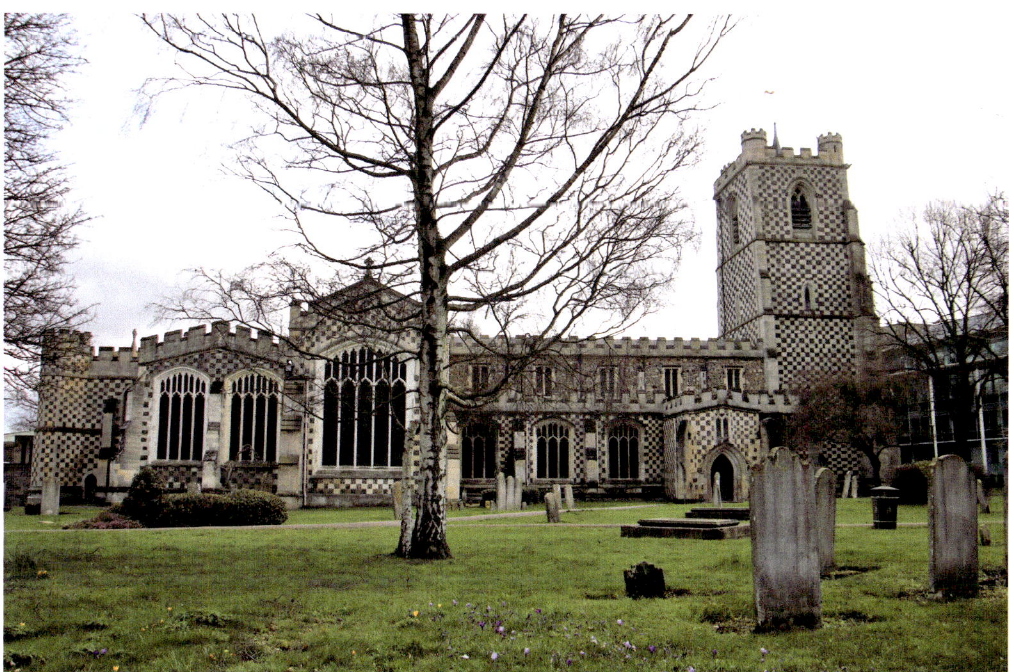

Luton, St Mary's Church.

sitting. As a politician he was High Sheriff of Bedfordshire and Buckinghamshire and Member of Parliament for Luton.

In 1461, the chapel off the north transept was renamed the Wenlock Chapel and John's father is one of three people interred there. Off the south transept is the Hoo Chapel which now acts as the organ loft.

The church houses a number of magnificent stained-glass windows, depicting scenes such as Adam and Eve in the Garden of Eden and Enoch and Noah, to name but two. More recently the somewhat abstract 'Magnificat' window was installed in 1979, replacing one from the nineteenth century in poor condition. This 1979 work by Alan Younger is said to suggest Mary's 'outpouring of gratitude' and 'explosion of happiness'.

Several other churches lie within the town's boundaries, but none have the 'wow' factor evident when approaching St Mary's.

27. MARSTON MORETAINE, ST MARY

The large village, with a population of around 4,500, is situated on the former main road between Bedford and Milton Keynes, in the Marston Vale. Confusion surrounds the village's spelling, which takes its name originally from a French family. The alternative spelling of 'Moreteyne' is also widely used.

On approaching St Mary's, the visitor cannot fail to notice its striking battlements and that the church tower, unusually, stands apart from the church building. The tower stands approximately 20 metres from the north wall of the chancel, on a different alignment.

Legend has it that the tower is detached because of the work of the devil, who tried to steal the 20- metre-high tower. It was too heavy, however, and it is said

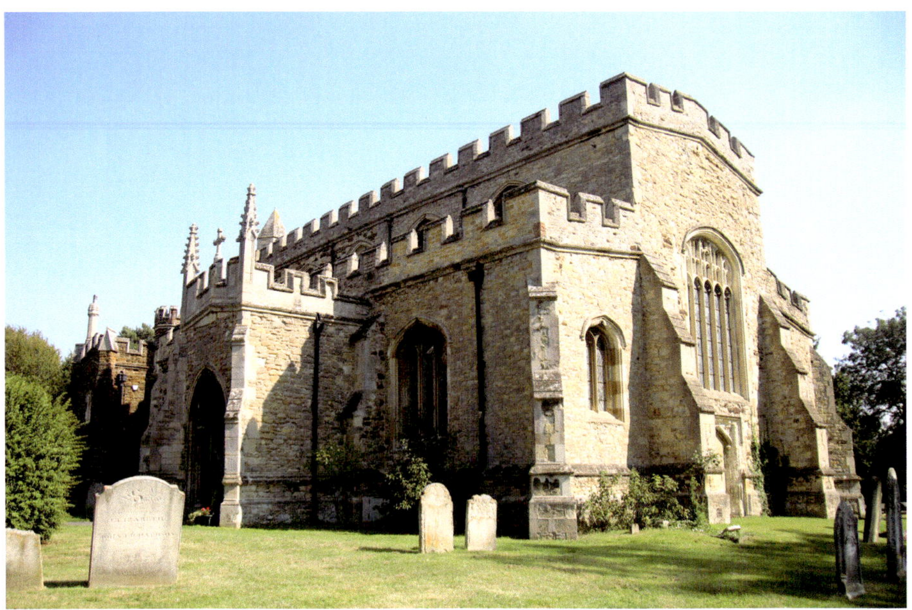

Marston Moretaine Church.

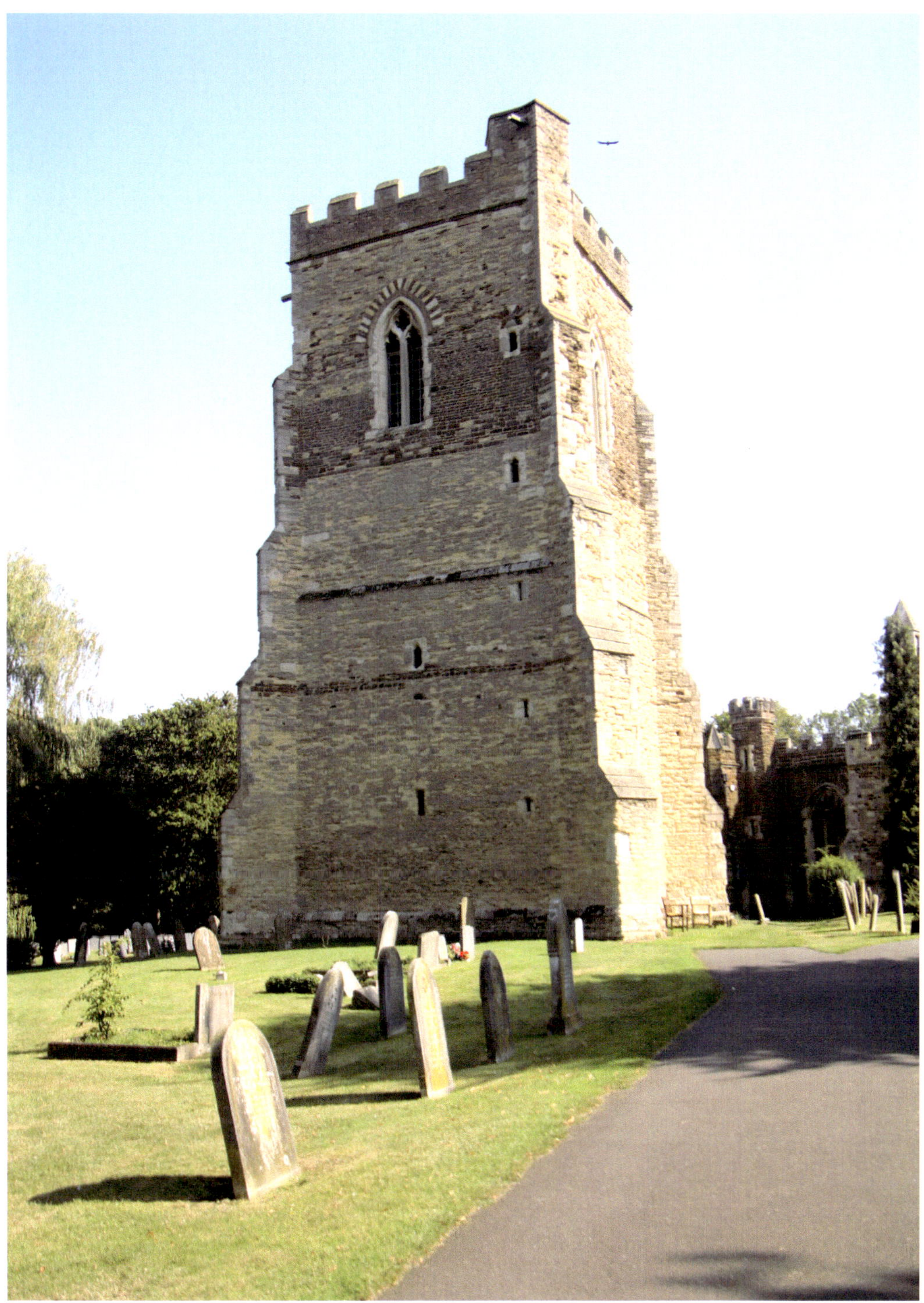

Detached tower, Marston Moretaine.

he dropped it where it stands today. Other local tales tell that it was once used as a watch tower, and a place of refuge in times of strife. The most compelling story entails the villagers' use of it to take refuge from the pillaging of the Vikings, whose longships sailed the River Great Ouse as far as Bedford. These stories simply add to the mystique surrounding the church's history.

The church dates back to around 1340, being completely rebuilt around a hundred years later by Thomas Reynes, the local fifteenth-century Lord of the Manor. The position of Lord of the Manor was later held by a Speaker of Elizabeth I's House of Commons, Sir Thomas Snagge, whose elaborate tomb memorial is to be found inside the church's Reynes Chapel.

Historically, the old village lay to the south and access was therefore more convenient to parishioners approaching the church from that direction. This south porch is now blocked externally, with the north porch added later as the village itself expanded to the north.

The church has many interesting features, including the 'Doom' painting above the chancel arch. This depiction of the Last Judgment is one of the country's latest, dating from the beginning of the sixteenth century. It was not fully uncovered and subsequently cleaned until the 1960s.

Today, St Mary's Church in Marston Moretaine has pastoral oversight for the neighbouring community of Lidlington, where a single congregation of Anglican, Baptist and Methodist worshippers make use of a single chapel there.

28. Meppershall, St Mary

With a population of around 2,000 residents, the hilltop village of Meppershall is close to the small town of Shefford, with which it shares a benefice. Meppershall lies close to the border with Hertfordshire and was part of that county until transfer to Bedfordshire in 1844.

The church, which lies at the southern end of the village, dates back to the Normans. The original manor house is mentioned in the Domesday Book and was owned by the De Meppershall family.

The church of St Mary's dates back to the twelfth century, with the tower being the oldest part. Its layout is unusual in that the tower is at the centre of its cruciform shape. It is possible that this original tower's position was altered by Sir Arthur Bloomfield in the 1870s. A new transept and chancel could have been built around the tower at this time. Aisles were added on both sides of the nave which was completely rebuilt at the same time. This well-travelled man was a prolific architect who specialised in both church building and restoration.

Further renovation work has occurred regularly since then. In particular, the south transept now holds St John's Chapel, which was restored after the Second World War to commemorate the local men who gave their lives.

The church today has had to come to terms with the village's rapid expansion. It is entirely possible for a newcomer to live in the village and not know where the church is situated, being at one end of it and not the centre. It has endeavoured to engage with its parishioners by their 'Welcome and Outreach' philosophy. Consequently, the church actively engages with the village community in a variety of ways. They deliver 'welcome' bags to new arrivals in the village as well as

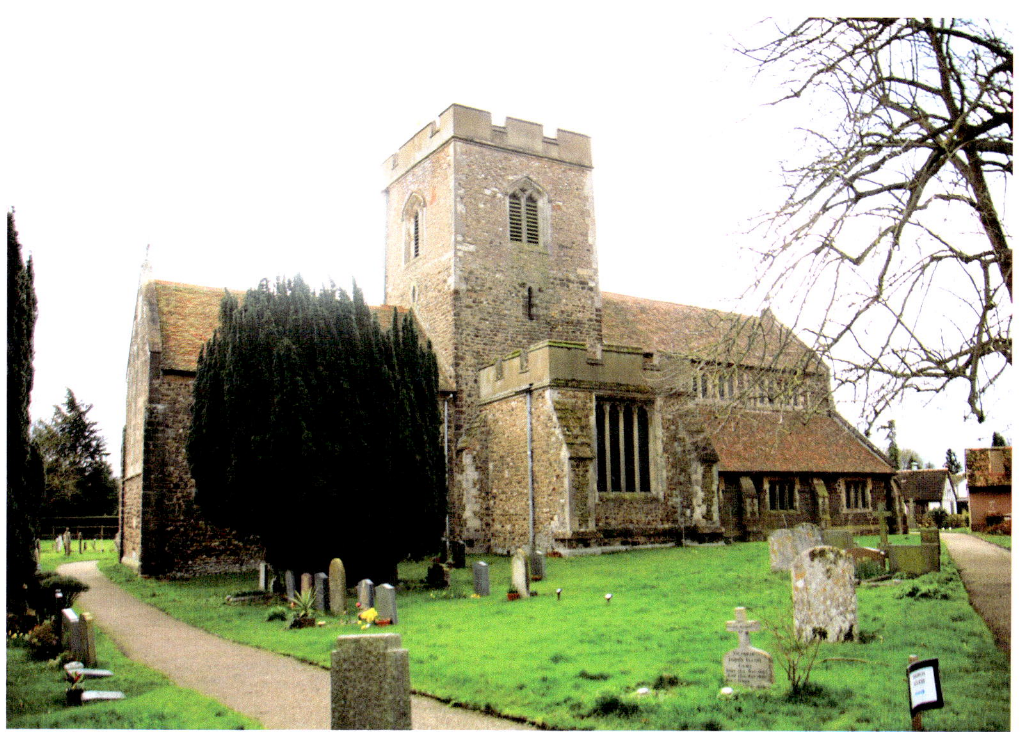

Meppershall Church.

Christmas cards to every household. In addition, they host a variety of events throughout the year, notably an annual scarecrow festival with its finale taking place at the church.

29. NORTHILL, ST MARY THE VIRGIN

The village of Northill lies around 7 miles southeast of Bedford, with a local population of around 350. At the centre of the village lies Northill pond, the pub, the green and St Mary's Church.

Northill is a large parish of over 4,000 acres. The River Ivel forms the eastern boundary of the parish with Northill itself lying on the western side. The village takes its name from the Saxon Gifle tribe, who inhabited the Ivel valley around AD 477. It was known to be called North Givle and nearby Southill referred to as Sud Givele. The Saxons are thought to have driven the Brits westwards with a watch hill at Old Warden. Today, St Mary's Church, Northill, forms a benefice with Caldecote and Old Warden.

It is almost certain that a Saxon church, followed by a Norman church, stood on the site of the present building during the fourteenth century. The church walls are constructed of ironstone and Totternhoe clunch. The nave is built of dressed stone, whilst the chancel is made up of pebbles and rubble. This poor, inferior construction work may well be due to the Black Plague, which interrupted the building work and killed many master masons.

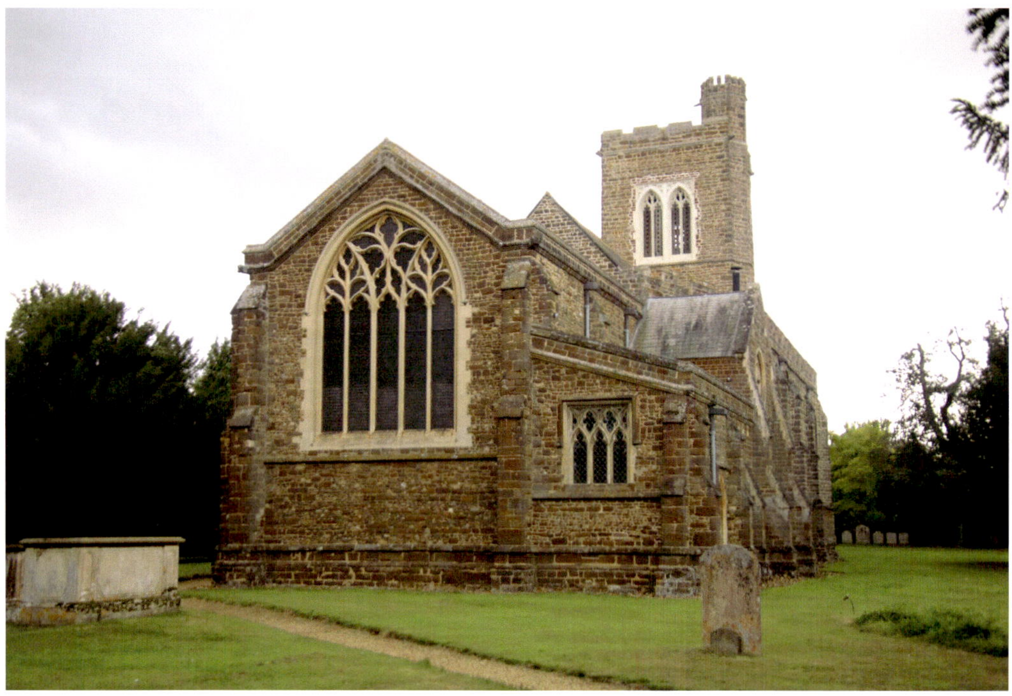

Northill Church.

Like most churches, it has had many additions and alterations. The structural history of the church is well documented. Northill has a very detailed set of churchwardens' accounts dating from 1561 to 1927. There are also a set of inventories of church goods from 1605 to 1841. The latter are fairly detailed right down to the mention of the church organ being installed in 1590 and some of its pipes being sold that same year.

These detailed records reveal anomalies as to the origin of the church clock. The parish chest documents note the clock was installed in the tower in 1663, and local legend infers it was made by Thomas Tompion, a famous watch and clock maker who was born locally. However, the churchwardens' accounts make no mention until 1708, by which time Tompion had left the area. He moved to London in 1670 and died in 1718. His father was both a churchwarden and local wheelwright in 1665. Although the dates in the various accounts don't seem to tally, it remains a matter of some intrigue as to whether it is a Tompion clock or not.

The church is noted for its fine stained-glass windows. Its royal coat of arms is that of King Charles II, to be found on one of these. It was designed by John Oliver and was commissioned in 1664 by the Worshipful Company of Grocers who were a patron of the church, their arms appearing next to the King's. John Oliver was perhaps better known for his employment in the rebuilding of London following the Great Fire of 1666. The font and its canopy are also noteworthy.

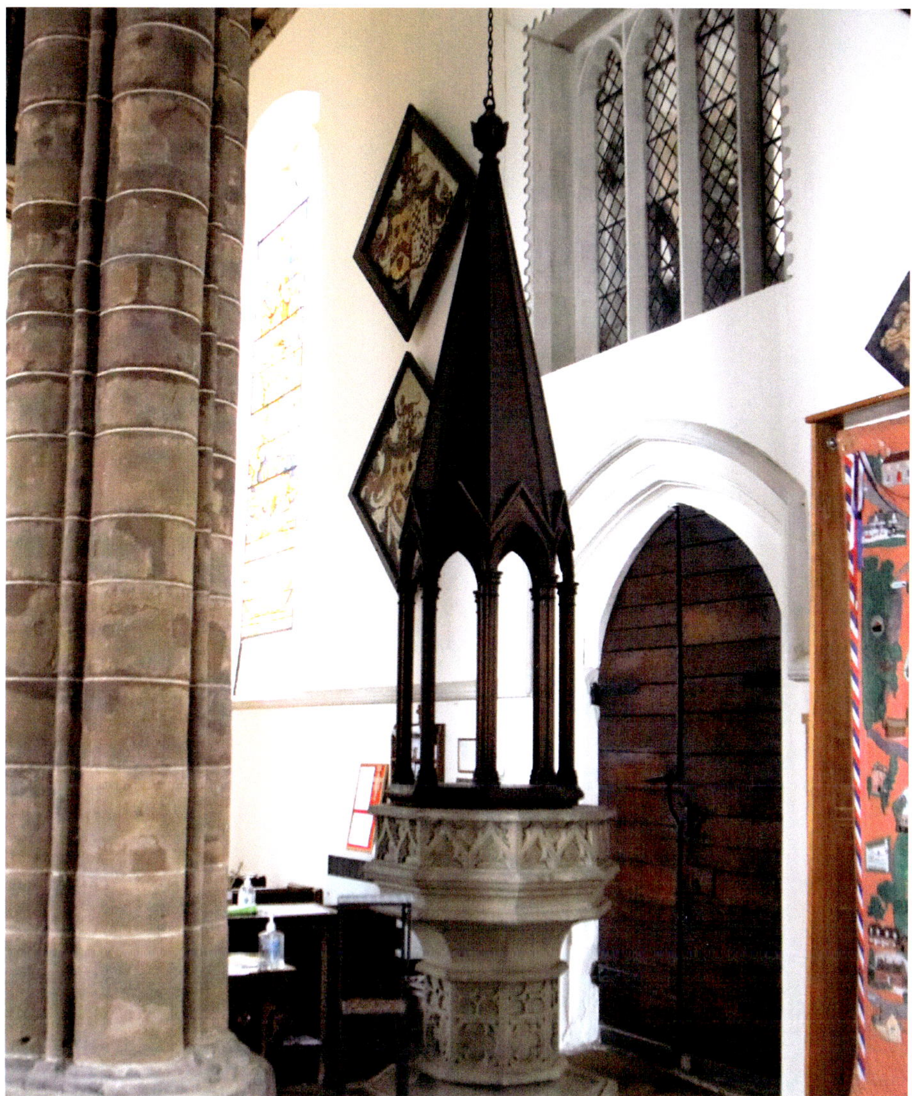

Font, Northill.

30. OLD WARDEN, ABBEY CHURCH OF ST LEONARD

St Leonard's lies around 7 miles south-east of Bedford. The Central Bedfordshire village of Old Warden has a population bef just over 300. This parish forms a benefice along with Northill and Caldecote. The church of St Leonard's dates back to the early twelfth century, becoming a Grade I listed building in 1966. The present structure dates from the thirteenth century, with a number of additions over the ensuing 300 years. The more recent history of the church is dominated by two local landowning families, namely the Ongleys and the Shuttleworths.

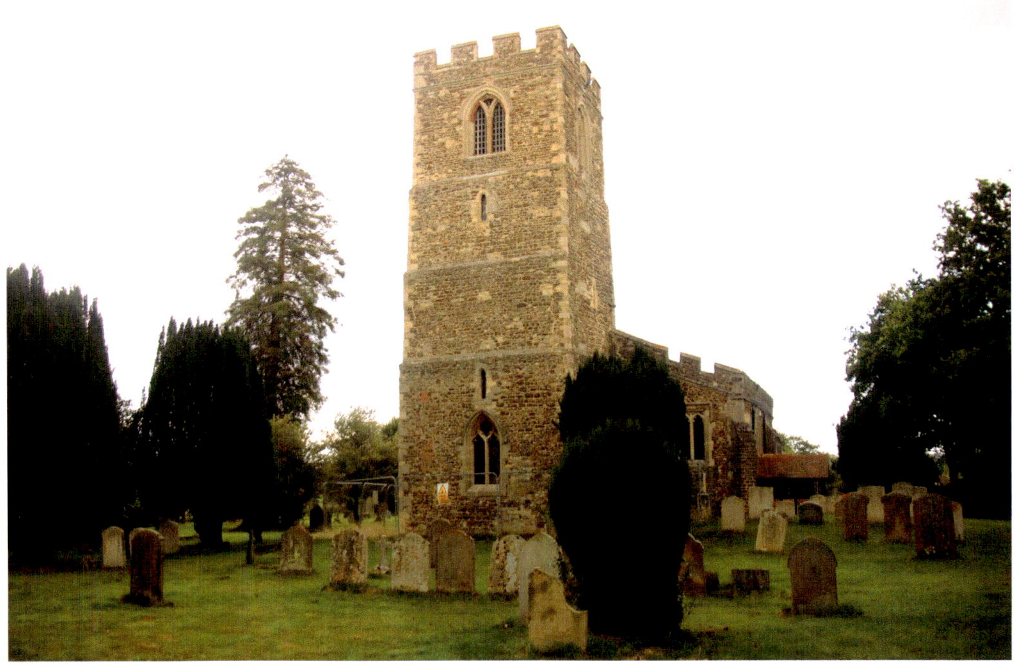

Old Warden Church.

The Ongley family had purchased the Old Warden estate from the Bolingbroke family in 1700.

The church was originally constructed mainly from brown cobblestones and limestone facings, with later additions in red brick. In the mid-nineteenth century the ornate wooden carvings were given to the church by Robert Henley-Ongley, the 3rd Baron Ongley of Old Warden. A number of these were stolen at the end of the last century and, sadly, never recovered.

Most of these carvings were brought from Belgium, France and Italy, including a number of panels from the private chapel of Anne of Cleves, the fourth wife of Henry VIII. These panels can be identified by their carved centrepiece bearing the initials 'AC' together with the crown. The wooden box pews are also distinctive, being topped with elaborate carvings of snakes – or serpents, one slithering to the east, the other to the west. The wooden pulpit was bought in Edinburgh by Frank Shuttleworth. It is thought to be eighteenth-century Flemish and shows Jesus with children and the Woman of Samaria.

In 1872, the Shuttleworth family purchased the estate from the Ongleys and became the principal landowners within the parish, with evidence of the history of both families to be found in the churchyard.

The Shuttleworth family have been responsible for most of the windows being filled with stained glass to commemorate the passing of loved ones as well as marking family marriages and monarch coronations. The large box pew at the top of the nave opposite the pulpit was the Shuttleworth family pew.

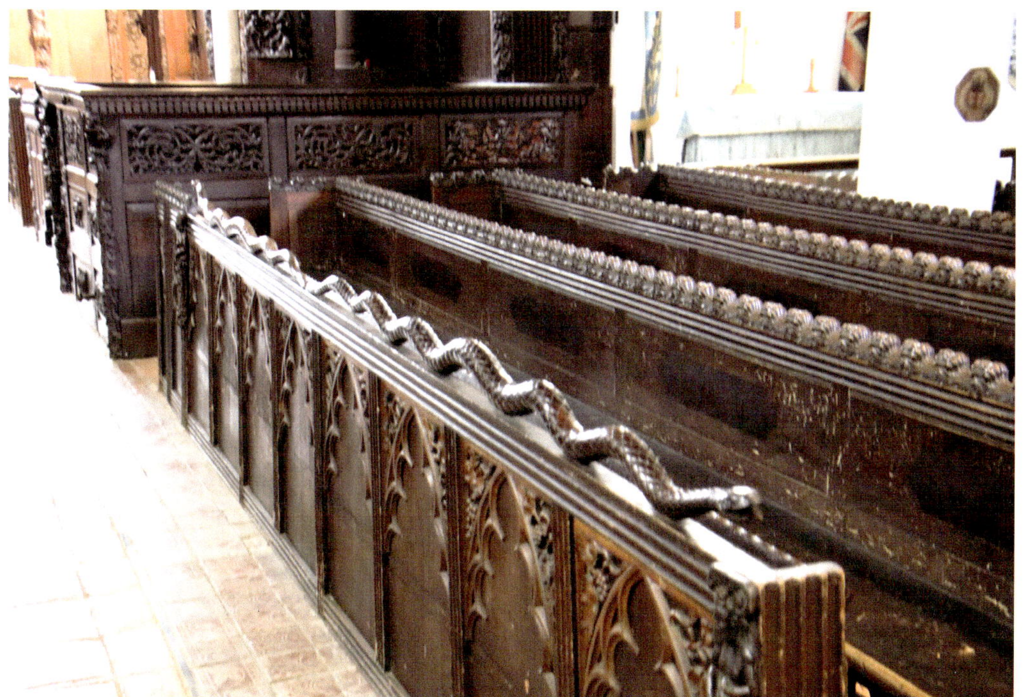

Pews, Old Warden.

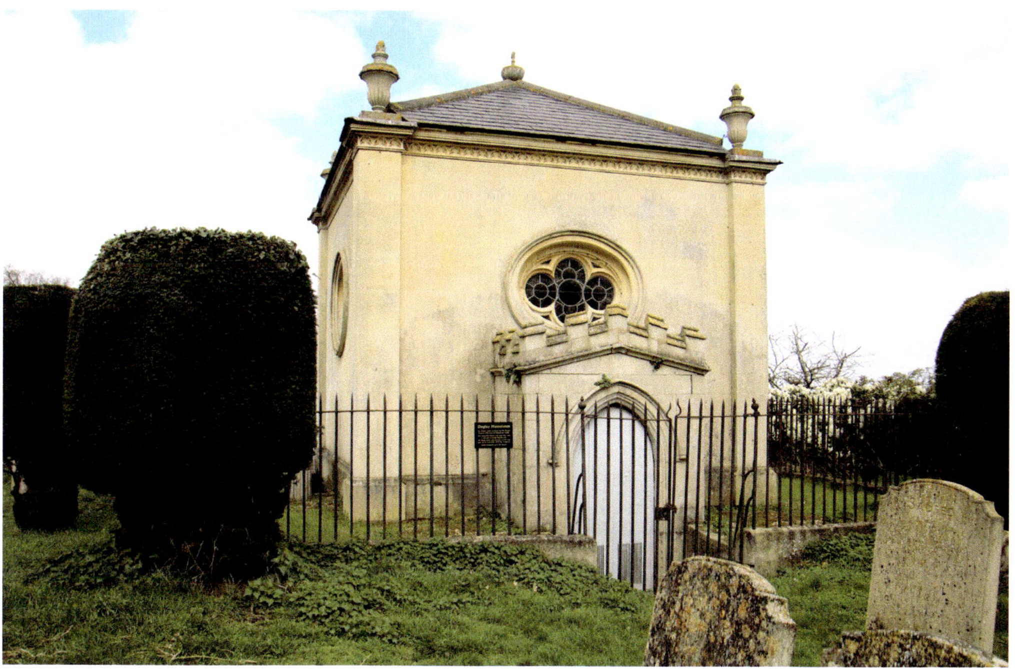

Ongley mausoleum, Old Warden.

Visiting Old Warden church gave us extra pleasure because John Sumner, our 'navigator', has vivid childhood memories of visits here some eighty-five years ago when his father used to be a visiting preacher to St Leonard's.

31. PAVENHAM, ST PETER

The village of Pavenham lies around 6 miles to the northwest of the county town of Bedford. It has a population of approximately 750. St Peter's is located to the north of the village on the road to Felmersham. Its position on a slope above this road gives an even more impressive view of this imposing structure.

Its spire is particularly unusual. Often referred to as a broach spire, it is an octagonal structure sitting on top of a square tower. Each triangular face of this spire is termed a broach. It is an excellent example of early English architecture, dating back some 600 years.

The church's exterior features a number of intriguing corbels. One of these, in particular, caught our eye. By a doorway at the foot of the tower is one fine example depicting a dog's head, leaving us to ponder whether it was the stonemason's pet!

On entering the church there are many unusual features. With only one small stained-glass exception, the remainder of the plain, clear windows give an abundance of natural light. This more than compensates for another unusual feature which is the Jacobean dark oak panelling. This ornately carved panelling extends to just above head height throughout the church except for the east wall of the transept.

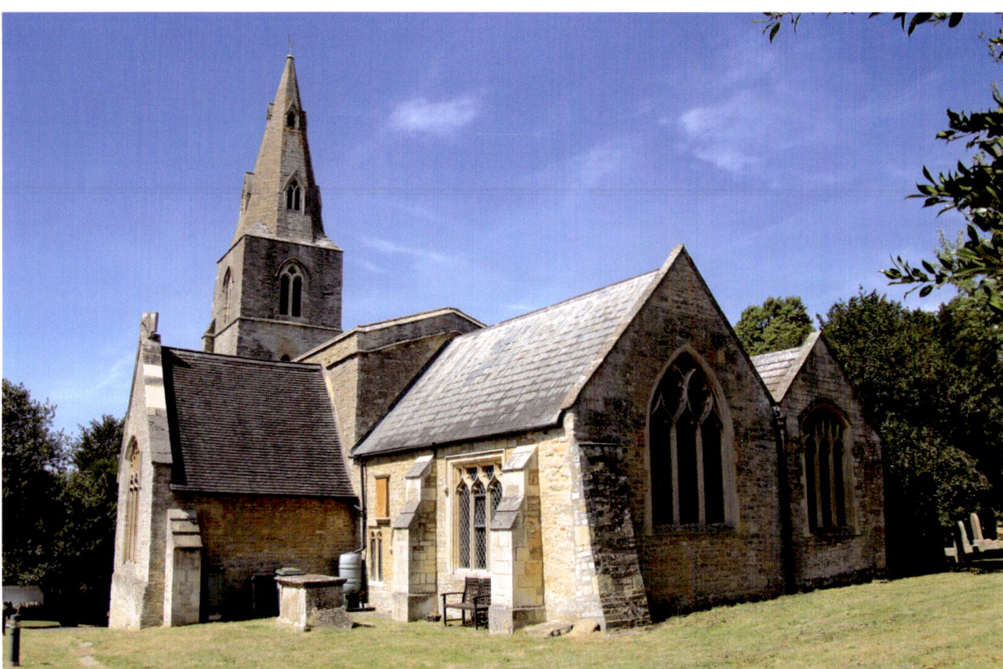

Pavenham Church.

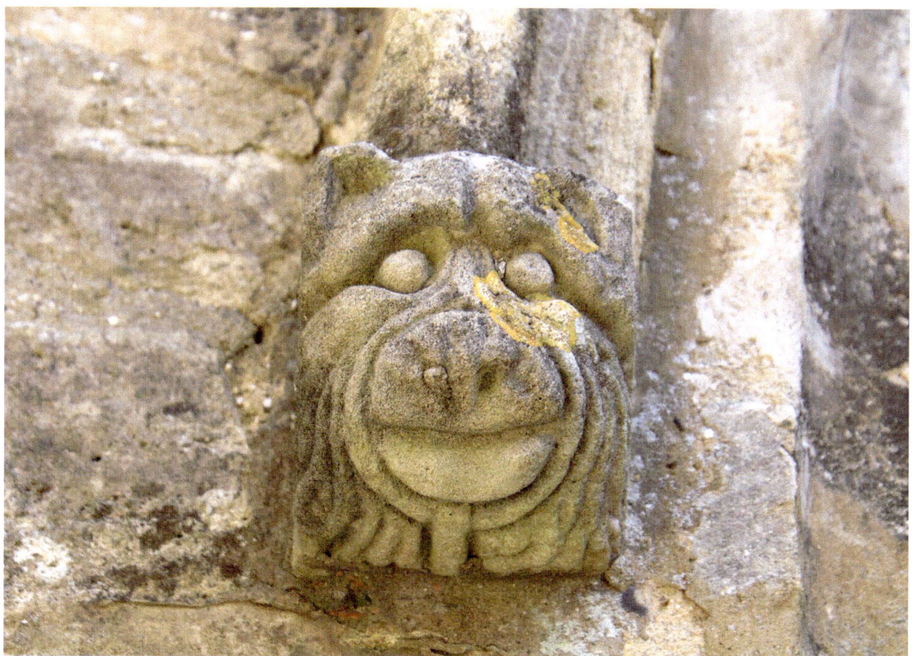

Corbel, Pavenham.

In 1840, local churchwarden Thomas Abbott Green inherited Pavenham Bury, a now demolished nearby country house. As a timber merchant, he was responsible for collecting this seventeenth-century carved panelling from both home and abroad. The latter is thought to have been found in French and Flemish abbeys.

This panelling extends to include the pulpit and surrounding area. Some of the panels depict domestic scenes, for example a hen tucked under the arm of one of the figures and another carrying a musical instrument. It is unlikely they were originally intended for a place of worship.

The church of St Peter's in Pavenham forms a benefice (MPT) with All Saints Church in Milton Ernest and St Peter's in Thurleigh.

32. PERTENHALL, ST PETER

Pertenhall is an ancient parish located 7 miles northwest of St Neots, 10 miles north of Bedford, in Bedfordshire just west of the Cambridgeshire border. It has a small population of around 200.

The church of St Peter is situated off the B660 Keysoe to Kimbolton road in the middle of the hamlet of Pertenhall. It stands in a wooded churchyard which is accessed via a track.

The church building dates from the beginning of the twelfth century at the end of the Norman era. Its first incumbent was employed in 1154. There is evidence that the chancel was rebuilt in the thirteenth century and a chapel added to the north side of the chancel a century later.

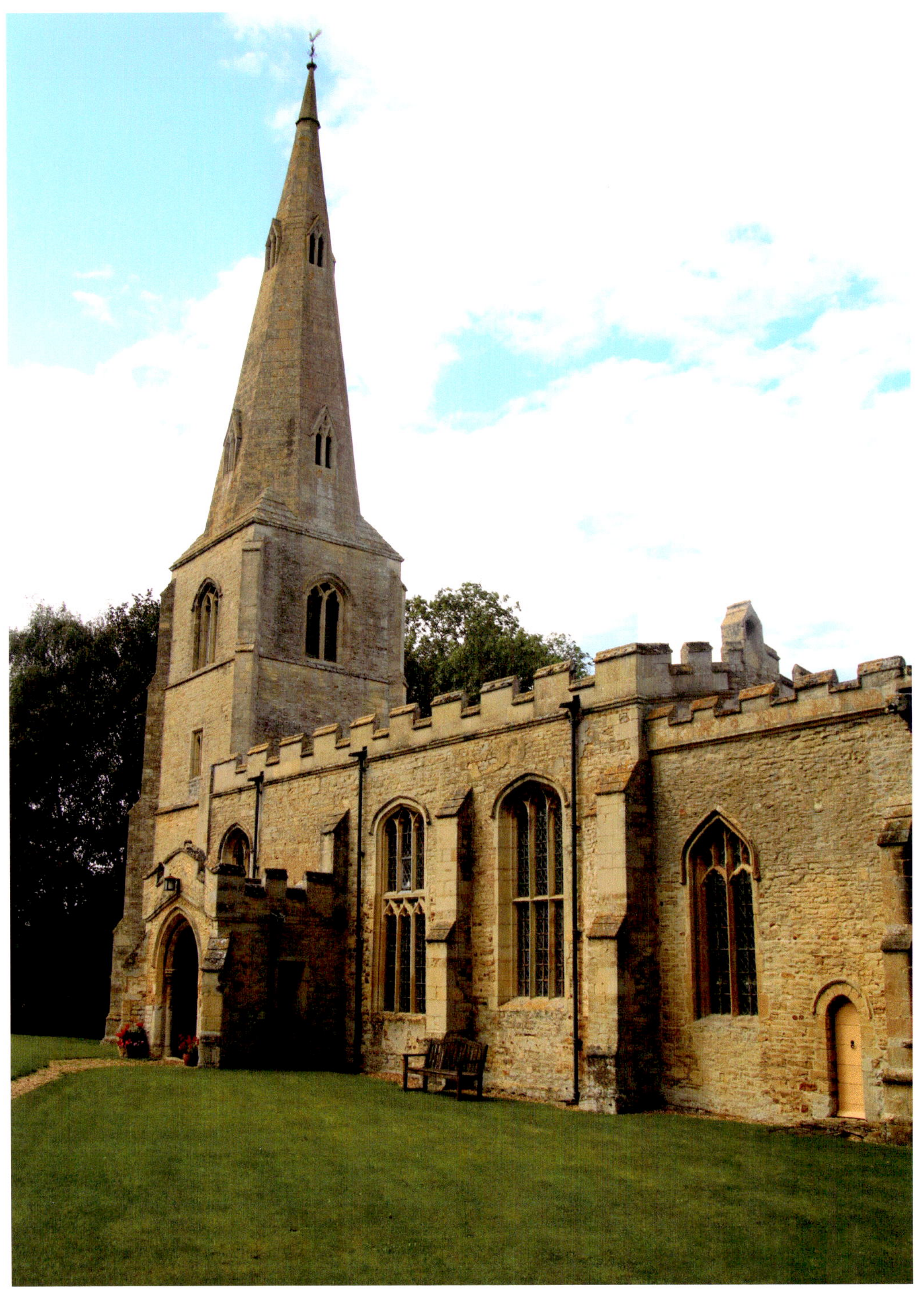

Pertenhall Church.

Further rebuilding took place in the fifteenth century with the erection of a west tower, spire, south porch and aisle. The majority of the church is embattled and its perpendicular west tower has four stages and a broach spire, making it quite spectacular.

On entering the church, one's eyes are drawn towards the rich tracery of the rood screen, which has retained some of its colour for more than 500 years. It is thought that some of the pews are of the same era as this screen, whilst others are from the seventeenth century.

The nave has three bay arcades dating back to 1190. On the south wall of the nave there is a small seventeenth-century memorial marble tablet to Rolt family members. Oliver Cromwell's youngest daughter, Mary, who was married to Edward Rolt, is mentioned on this tablet.

St Peter's of Pertenhall is part of the Stodden benefice. This benefice also includes All Hallows Church, Dean; St Mary Magdalene, Melchbourne; St Mary's, Shelton; St Nicholas, Swineshead; and St Mary's, Yelden.

33. PODINGTON, ST MARY

Podington village, with a population of almost 500, lies around 10 miles to the northwest of Bedford, close to the county boundary with Northamptonshire. The church sits in the middle of the village, on the High Street. It dates back to Norman times, with parts, including the chancel, still remaining from the twelfth century.

Entering the church via a heavy oak door, the church's connection with the Orlebar family soon becomes obvious. This family owned nearby Hinwick

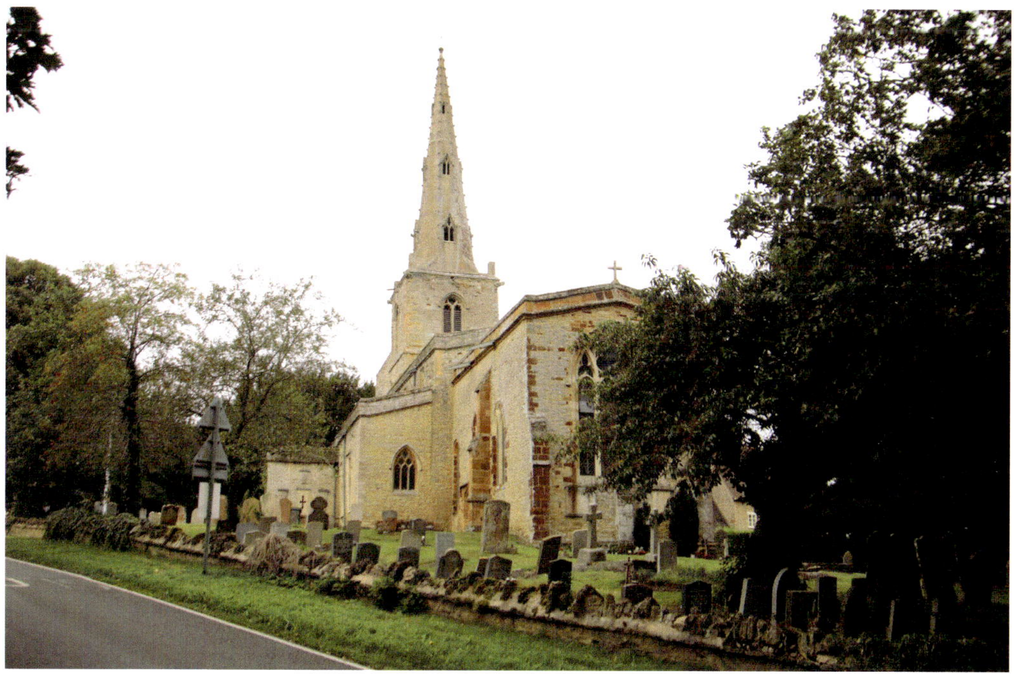

Podington Church.

House from the early 1700s until around twenty-five years ago. Amongst other family members, it is the final resting place of Richard Orlebar, High Sherriff of Bedfordshire in 1721, and his wife, Diana Astrey, who was a culinary writer of her day. Amongst the five funereal hatchments restored and handsomely displayed high in the church chancel is one to a member of the family.

The Orlebar Chronicles, a twentieth-century document covering a wealth of local and family history between the sixteenth and eighteenth centuries, reveal the fate of one of St Mary's vicars, John Henmarche. Together with abbot Robert Hobbes, the pair were hanged at Woburn, having been charged with 'manyfold crymes, enormities and high treson' in 1537.

A glance around the church brings one's gaze to the impressive nineteenth-century pipe organ. The 92nd Bombardment Group was stationed a couple of miles from the village during the Second World War. This group's Memorial Association has been responsible for the restoration of this organ. It has been cleaned and renovated to ensure its 'stops' are fully working. This organ is particularly noteworthy because the only electrical part is the bellows; all the 'stops' are sliding and made of wood.

Local parishioners believe the organ was built by a great grandfather of Andrew Lloyd Webber, very likely given the family's love of organ music. It is thought this

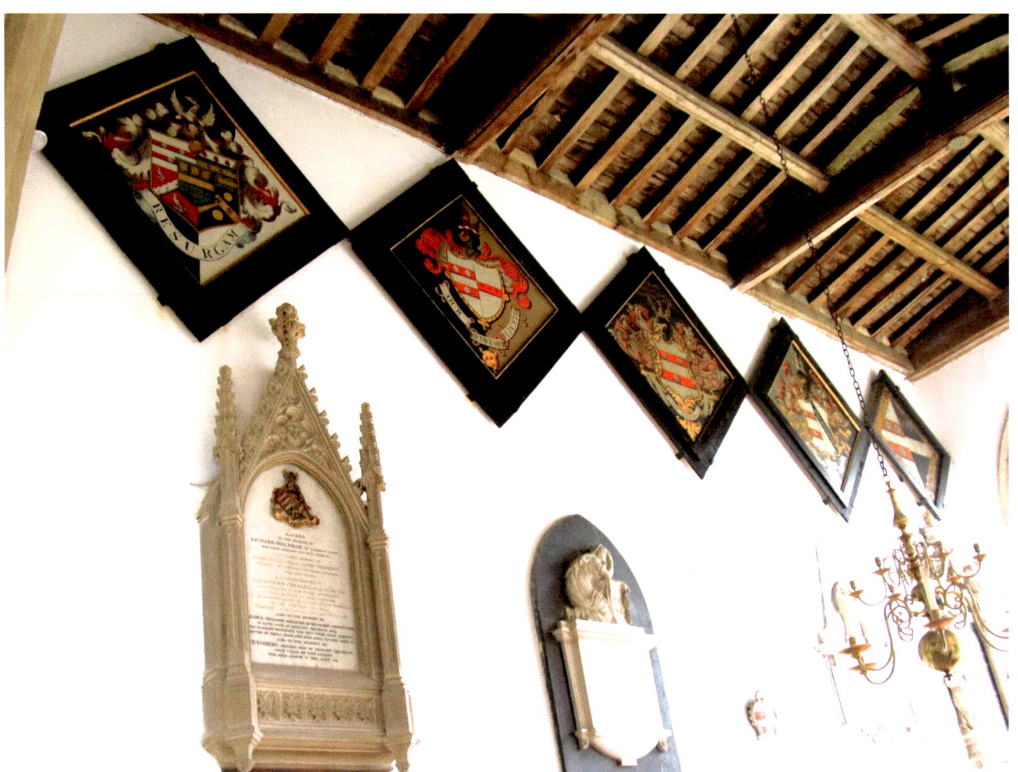

Hatchments, Podington.

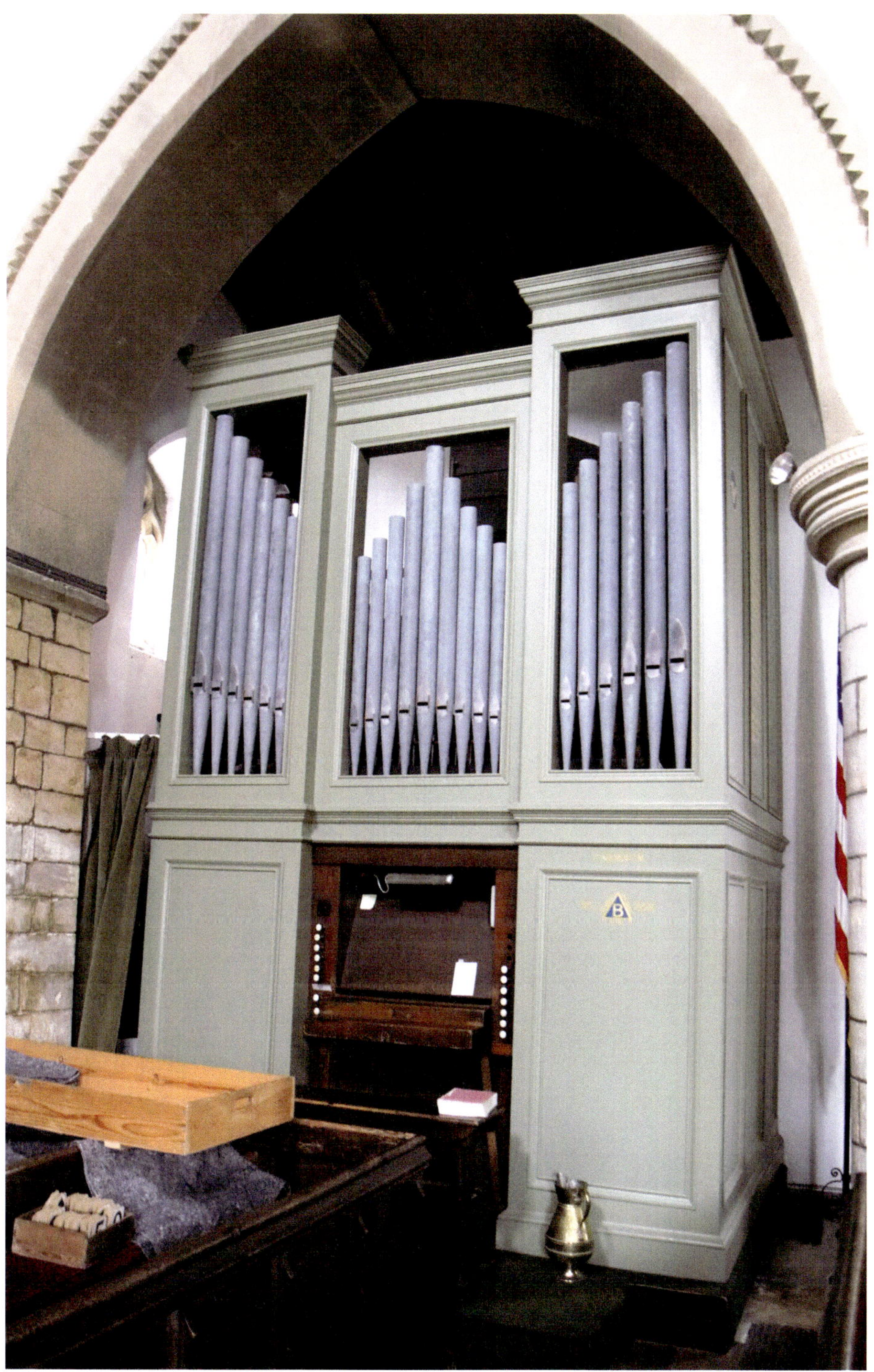

Organ, Podington.

 Churches of Bedfordshire

organ was originally housed at All Saints Church, Northampton, before a move to Hinwick House. Around five years later it was donated to the church.

This church at Podington forms part of the Chellington team ministry. This benefice encompasses seven parish churches together with Harrold United Reformed Church. Podington's sister Anglican churches are St Peter's in Harrold, St Mary's in Carlton, All Saints in Odell, All Saints in Turvey, St Mary the Virgin in Stevington, and St Lawrence's in Wymington.

34. POTTON, ST MARY

The churches of St Mary's, Potton, All Saints, Sutton, and St John the Baptist's, Cockayne Hatley, are all found in the same benefice, each with their own stories to tell.

The town of Potton, with a population of around 5,000, lies approximately 10 miles to the east of Bedford. It is pretty, embattled church sits high above the road, the site for worship dating back to the late eleventh century. It should be noted, however, that no part of the present building is older than the thirteenth century. The exterior of the church has not changed since the early sixteenth century when the southeast chapel was added.

One of its newest features is the stained-glass window in the south aisle. This was in celebration of 900 years of worship. The idea of this 900-year anniversary window was started by an anonymous donation of £900 by the suggester. Today, a book of thanks names all the people who contributed to this vibrant modern stained-glass window.

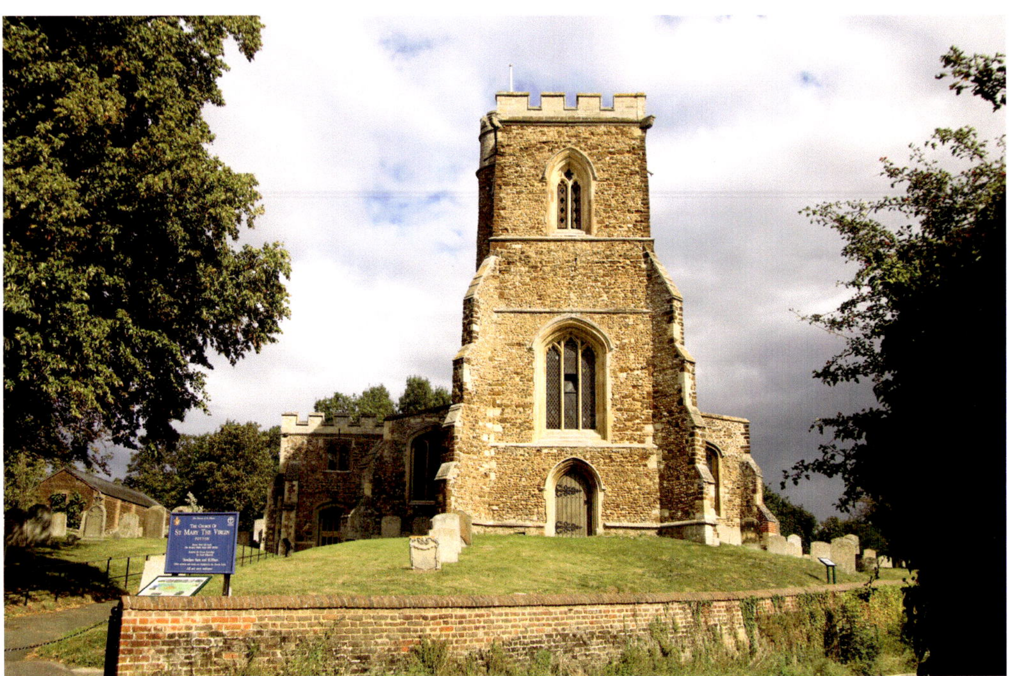

Potton Church.

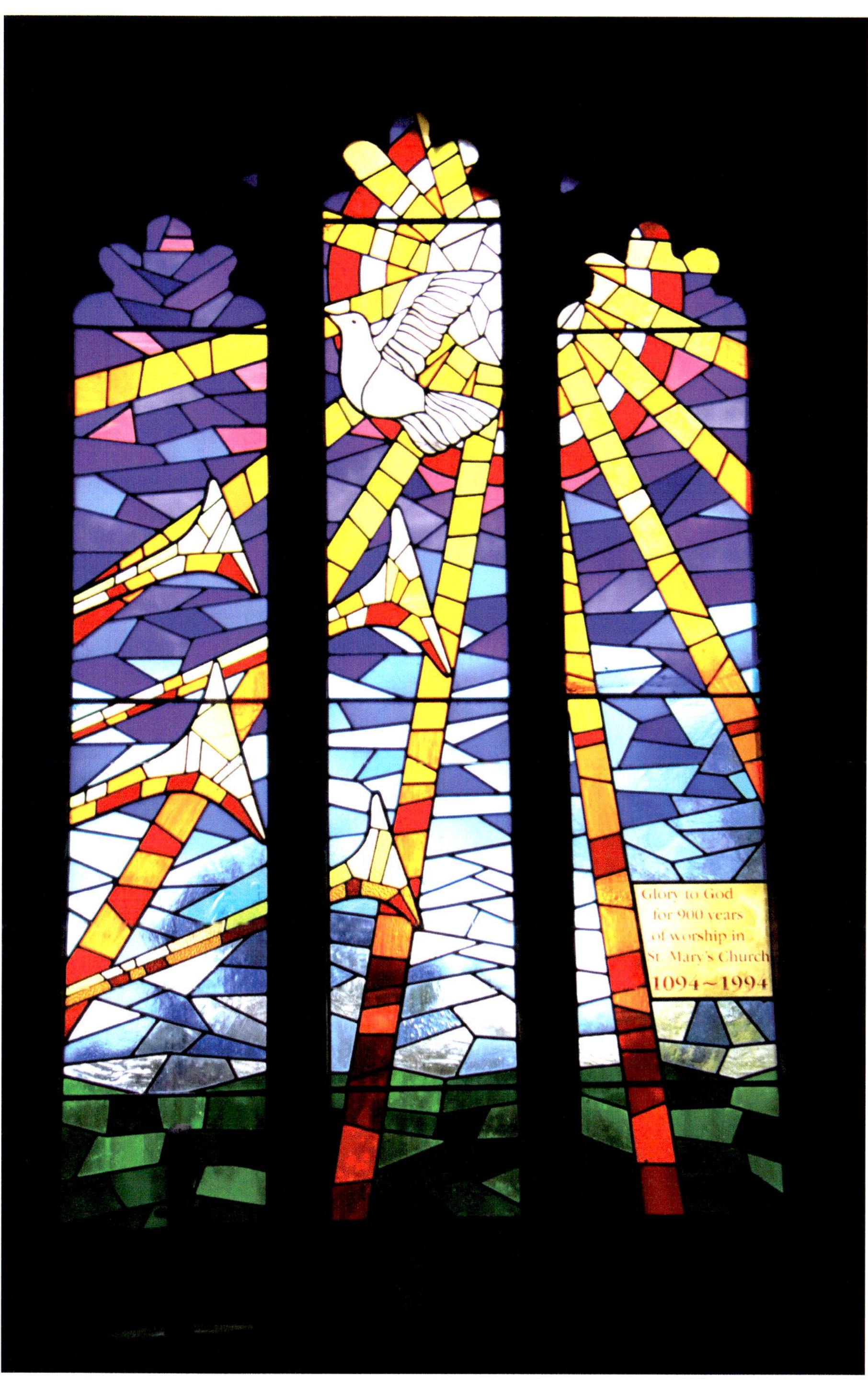

Window, Potton.

The village of Sutton lies close to Potton with All Saints Church, which dates from the twelfth century, at its centre. A priest's doorway, dating from the fifteenth century, is particularly intriguing due to its small size. The tower also dates from this period, although it was partially rebuilt in 1686.

Local folklore recalls one vicar in particular, Edward Drax Free, who 'ruled' the church from 1806 to 1830. This eccentric, larger-than-life clergyman gained a reputation for keeping pigs and other animals in the churchyard, stealing and selling the lead from the church roof, felling a large number of oak trees for timber as well as womanising. He even resisted his ousting by threatening his congregation with a gun. His reign eventually came to an end, and he got his comeuppance when he was run over by a horse and cart, which killed him!

Inside the church can be found monuments to the Burgoyne family, who were the lords of the manor for over 300 years. Sir John Burgoyne was a Member of Parliament in the late sixteenth century. His imposing marble monument stands at least 20 feet high and is complete with a black-headed dog at his feet. There are also examples of medieval graffiti surviving within the church.

The tiny community of Cockayne Hatley comprises a population of under 100. The church of St John the Baptist is set in a particularly rural location. The twelfth-century church stands close to the manor house. The Cockayne family purchased the 1,500-acre estate in 1407, which included the church itself, and were to be the owners for almost half a millennium.

A family descendant, The Hon. and Revd Henry Cockayne Cust, made it his mission to restore the church. As a well-travelled man, he was particularly interested in the woodwork from an abbey in Oignies, France. At the time,

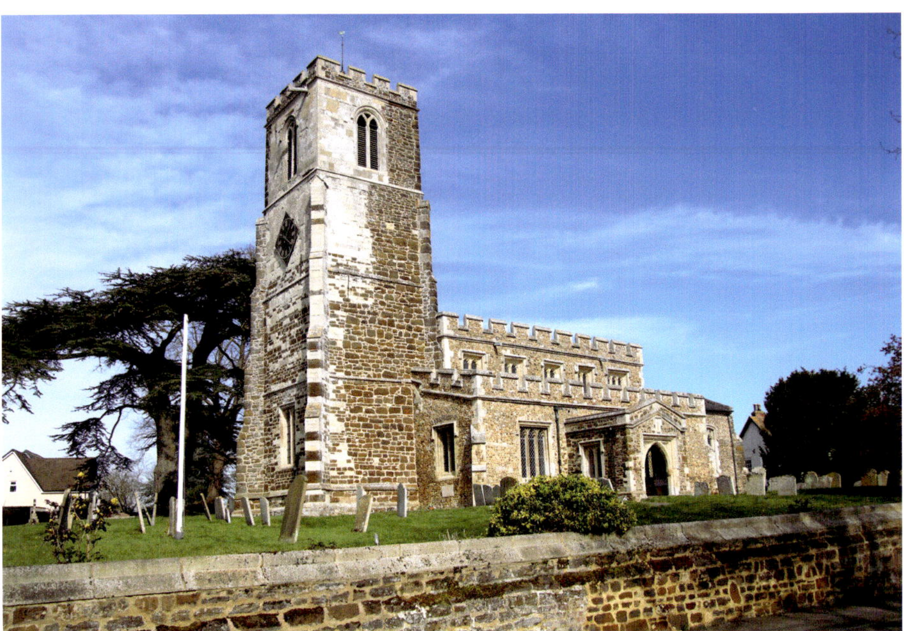

Sutton Church.

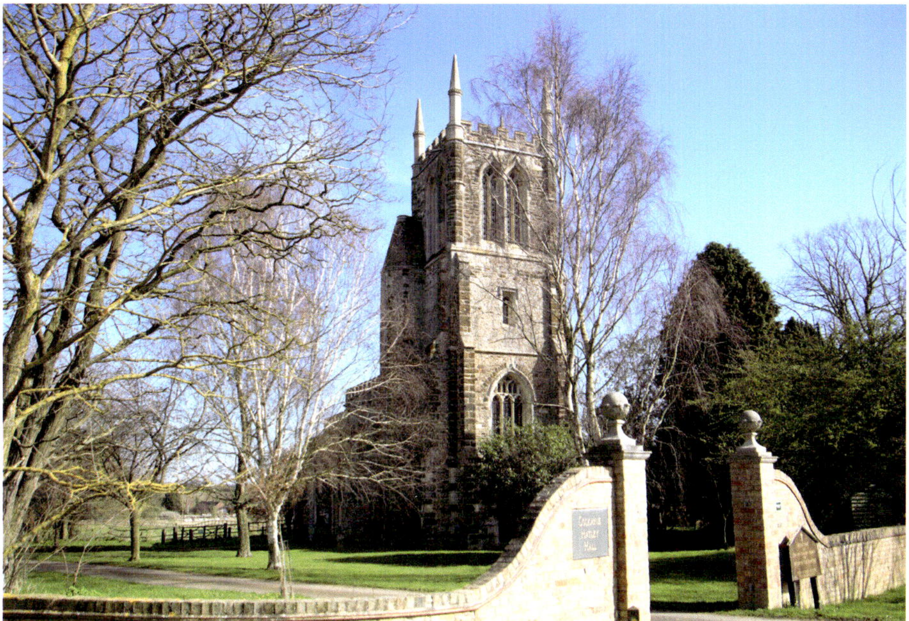

Cockayne Hatley Church.

Napoleon was responsible for sacking churches and monasteries, and sixteen large panels showing medallions of saints were amongst the items purchased and installed in St John the Baptist's Church.

The churchyard contains its own hidden gems. There is a monument to W. E. Henley, the poet who wrote 'Invictus'. His young daughter, Margaret, who died from meningitis aged five or six, is buried alongside her mother and father. She was the inspiration for the character in Sir J. M. Barrie's *Peter Pan* because her nickname for Barrie was 'Fwendy-wendy'. We believe this is also the first recorded use of the female forename Wendy in the UK.

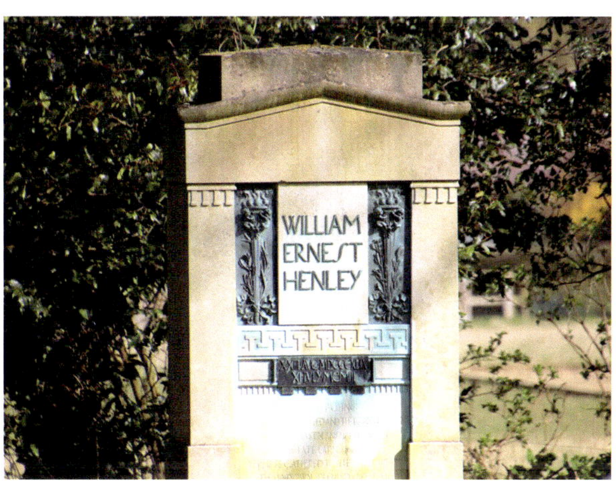

Monument, Cockayne Hatley.

35. PULLOXHILL, ST JAMES THE APOSTLE

Pulloxhill is an old Bedfordshire village. It is over 1,000 years old and still has a Norman church. It is 2 miles east of Flitwick, 8 miles north of Luton and 3 miles northeast of the Hertfordshire border. It has a population of around 1,000 and was originally referred to in the Domesday Book as 'Polochessie'. By 1205 it was known as Pollokeshill.

Pulloxhill was also an early home to the Bunyan family and close to where John Bunyan himself was arrested. In 1596, another villager, Elizabeth Ocle, was hanged in Bedford for practising witchcraft.

The church of St James the Apostle is situated to the west end of the village. What we see today was rebuilt in 1845/46 by local architect James Tacy Wing. The original church had fallen into ruin in the thirteenth century and the tower fell in the seventeenth century. The rebuilding was done in the original style and conformed to the original plans and incorporated many of the original features.

On entering the church, its interior strikes one as being plain Victorian, except for its chancel which still exhibits some of the original surviving features, such as a few ceiling beams and window traceries. The church is simple and dignified and suits the lovely village it serves. The views from the churchyard are some of the finest in the whole of Bedfordshire.

Today, Pulloxhill forms a benefice together with St John the Baptist, Flitton, and St James' in Silsoe.

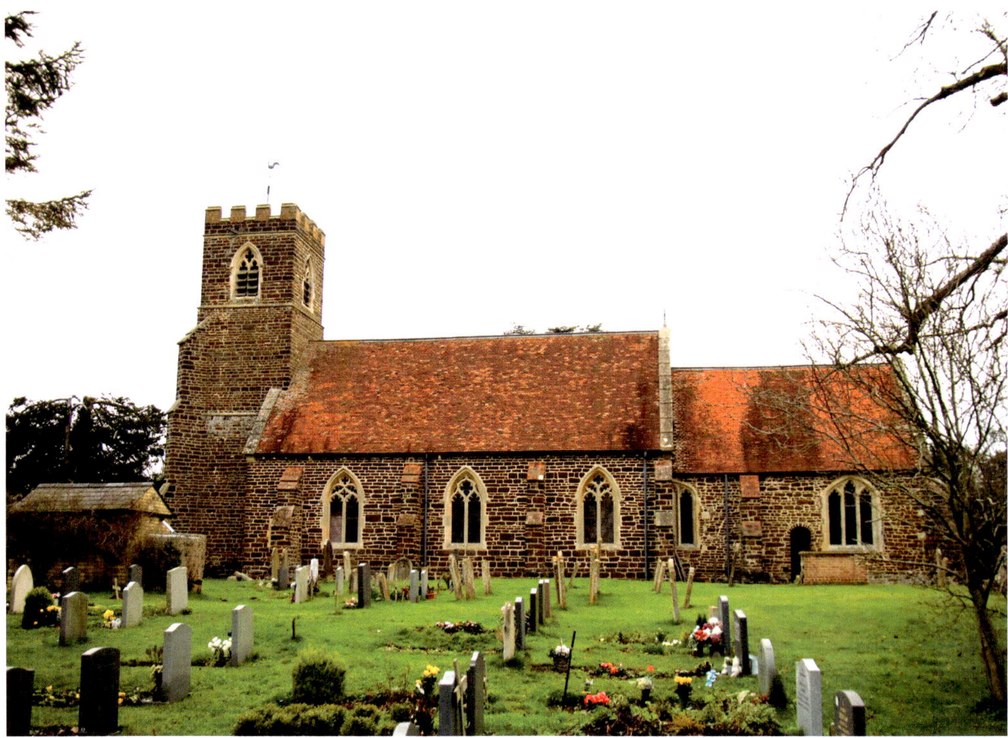

Pulloxhill Church.

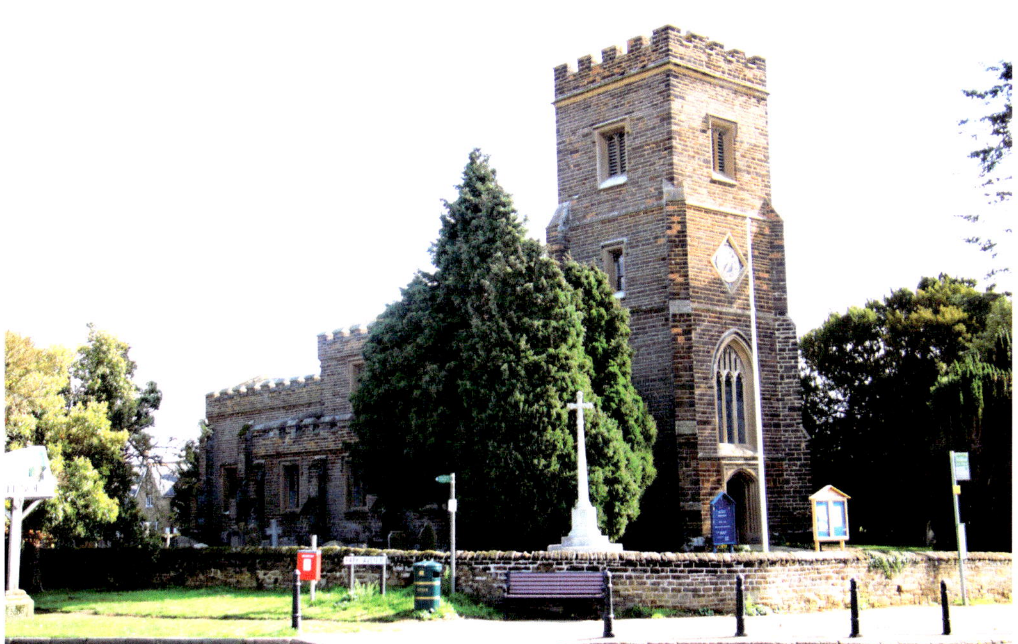

Silsoe Church.

36. RAVENSDEN, ALL SAINTS

The pretty village of Ravensden is located 3 miles northeast of Bedford and 4 miles southwest of the Cambridgeshire border, with a population of 2,000. All Saints Church is to the south of the main village between Bedford and Wilden. It is situated at the top of Church Hill and its quaint tower and tiny spire are a charming landmark.

The first record of the church is in 1166, however archaeological finds suggest an earlier place of worship was on the site in Saxon times. Much of the first recorded church was lost in a fire in the thirteenth century. The church has very little architectural distinctiveness. Its early patrons showed little or no interest in maintaining the actual building. The materials used in its fabrication demonstrate the church was cared for by locals using whatever materials they could. As a result, the church has a unique charm. It is built from coursed and uncoursed limestone, rubble, recycled Norman carvings, brown cobbles, Totternhoe clunch and recycled red tiles. The only remaining twelfth-century feature is the south wall of the nave. The chancel was widened in the fourteenth century and today's tower added in the fifteenth century.

Throughout history, All Saints Church has never been known as a rich church. Its survival is due to its dedicated parishioners. It has had more than its fair share of social dilemmas, caused by 'absent vicars' and documented disagreements surrounding the churchwarden in Victorian times.

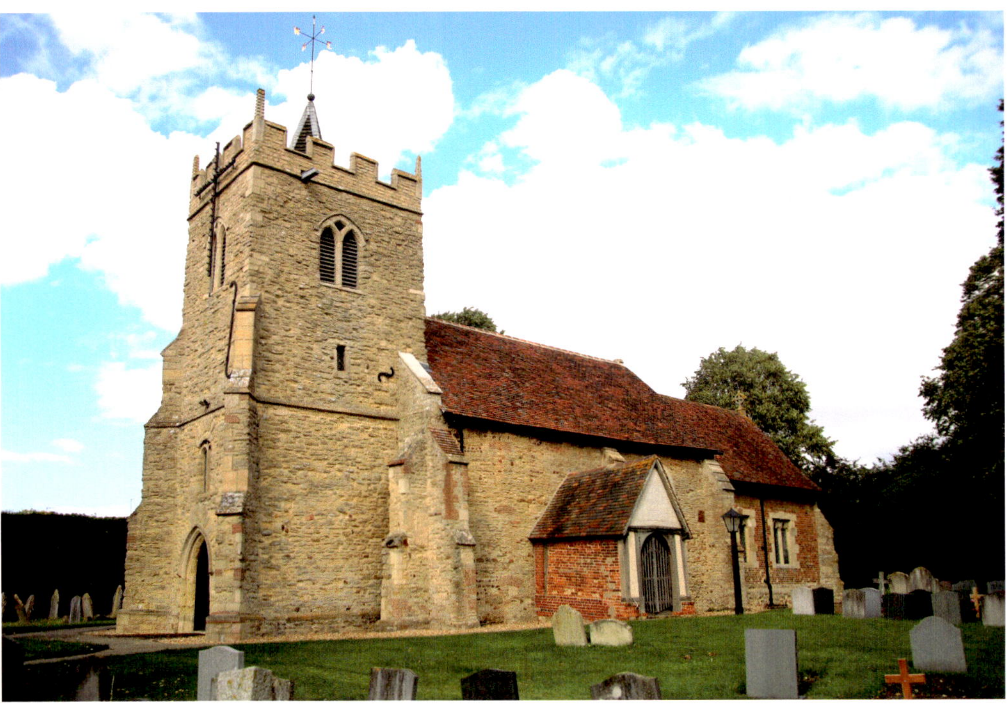

Ravensden Church.

Reports in the 1880s state clearly that the church was in a terrible state of disrepair. Eventually, the same churchwarden became involved and, in 1893, closed the church on what would today be known as health and safety grounds. He ripped out much of its interior and removed many books and Bibles stating that as he had paid for them, he could reclaim them. In 2007, a parishioner found one of these Bibles in a shop in Bedford, purchased it and placed it back in the church.

In 1900 and again in 1904, the church was given new vicars who worked hard to renovate the building and regain the trust of its parishioners.

On entering the church today, it is neat and tidy and well ordered. With individual chairs instead of pews and a mixture of plastered and natural rough stone walls, none of its past neglect and local squabbles are evident.

All Saints in Ravensden is in a benefice with St Nicholas, Wilden; St Denys, Colmworth; St Mary the Virgin, Keysoe; and St Dunstan's, Bolnhurst.

37. Ridgmont, All Saints

The village of Ridgmont lies close to junction 13 of the M1 motorway. It has a population of around 400. Today, it forms a benefice with St Botolph's, Aspley Guise, and St James', Husborne Crawley.

On approaching Ridgmont church today, the visitor is drawn firstly to the octagonal tower with spire and then, on closer inspection of the land around the building, there are no gravestones in evidence.

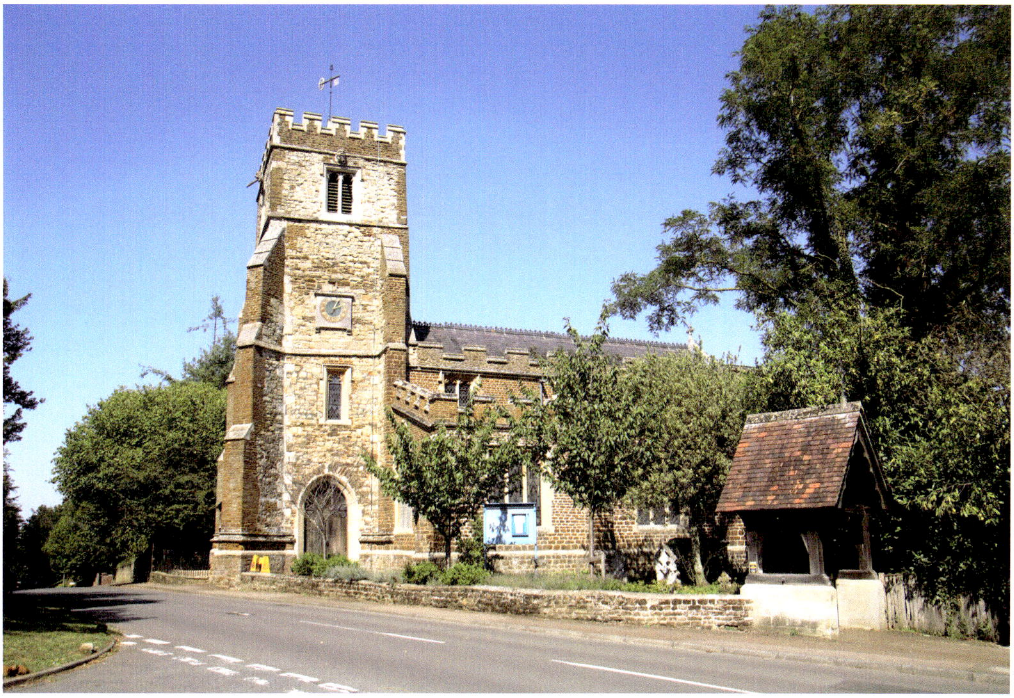

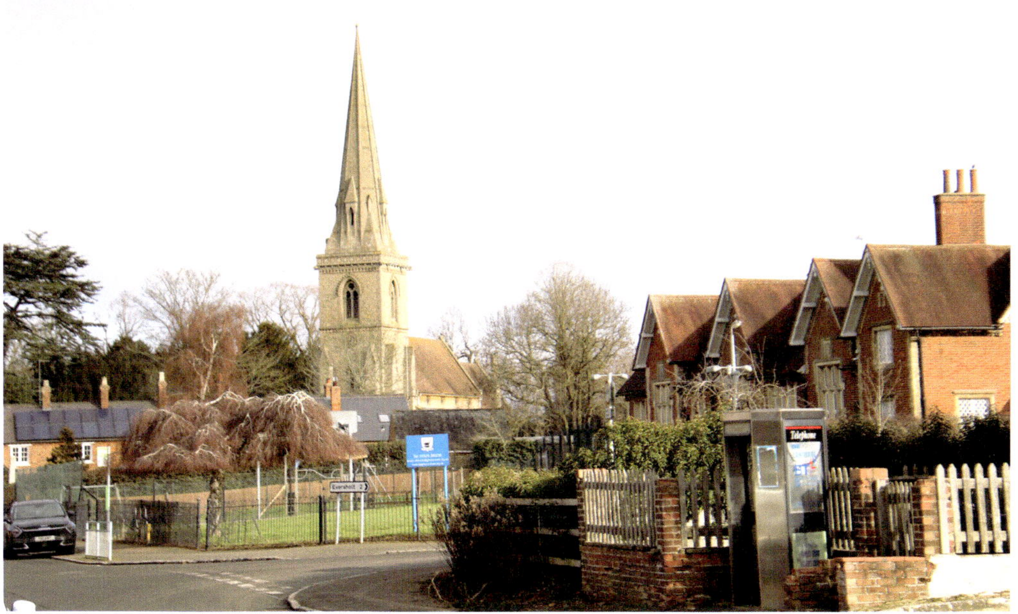

Husborne Crawley Church.

Ridgmont Church.

This is because today's church dates from the mid-nineteenth century. It was built to replace the original parish church of Sedgenhoe which had seen worship there since the twelfth century. That building was in a sad state of decay, and the decision was made to have a new, larger, building rather than attempt to repair the old. That said, village burials are undertaken on the old church site, accounting for the lack of gravestones at the new All Saints today.

The site at Sedgenhoe stands isolated around half a mile from the present church. Now roofless, the church site has drawn ghosthunters in recent times, who claim to have been in contact with the ghosts of young girls.

The 7th Duke of Bedford, Francis Russell, funded the building of the new All Saints Church and the foundation stone was laid in 1854 by the Duchess. It can be seen on the exterior wall at the east end of the chancel. Apart from some repair work, the church has changed little since those Victorian times.

The church is proud of its connection with the royal family over the years. Nina Cecilia Cavendish-Bentinck was christened here in 1862 when her father, Charles, was clergy of the church and encumbent of the nearby vicarage. He was great-grandfather to Queen Elizabeth II and great-great-grandfather to King Charles III.

Today, the lychgate allows entry to the church, with the well-lit path to the porch offering a warm welcome to the visitor, with a male and female face set in stone on either side of the porch. A glance both inside and out reveals further male and female faces.

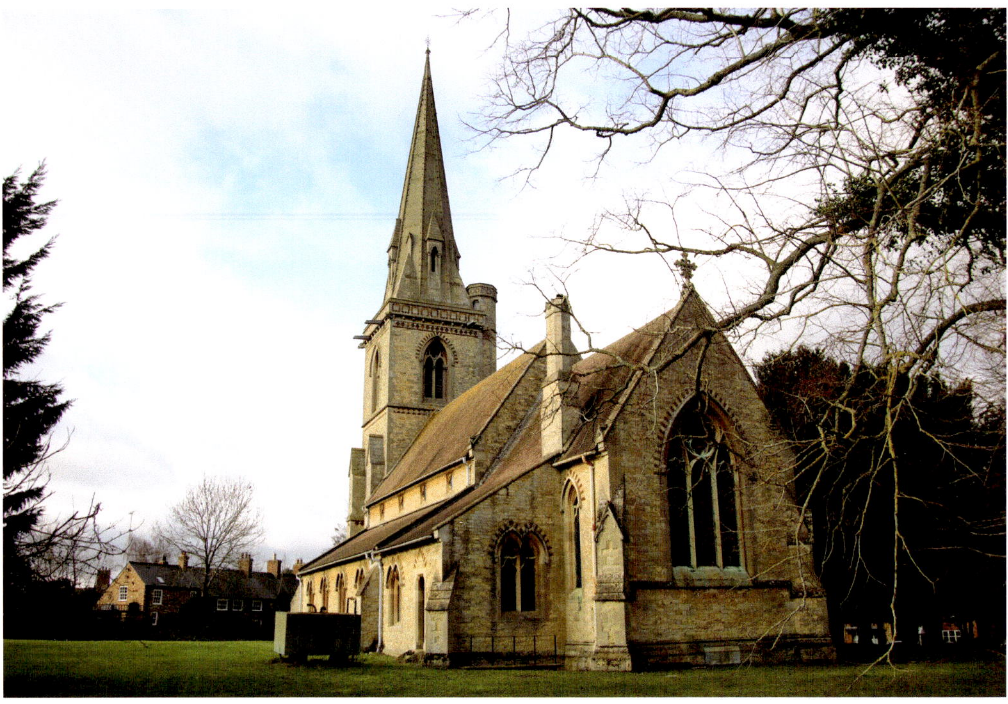

Ridgmont Church.

38. SANDY, ST SWITHUN

The Central Bedfordshire town of Sandy has a population of around 13,000 and lies on the A1, formerly the Great North Road. Even in Roman times, Sandy was a fairly large settlement positioned at a main road junction.

The church of St Swithun was constructed from locally quarried ironstone, although little of this original work remains. The church was extensively rebuilt in the nineteenth century under the guidance of the then vicar, Revd John Richardson, who came to Sandy in 1858 together with his wife, Ellen. The church was reopened in 1860, incorporating the existing tower but was larger, with a new roof and pews. For its day, the style of the windows and heads were elaborately ornate.

Sadly, after two years in the parish, John's wife Ellen died at the age of thirty-two, leaving him their three children. In 1861 he commissioned the south chancel window, which depicts six acts of mercy. Each of the six scenes focuses on the giver of mercy as a woman. He dedicated the window in memory of Ellen.

The church has a long association with two influential families, the Peels and the Pyms. These two families sat opposite each other for generations. Sir Robert Peel is remembered as being the prime minister who was the founder of the Metropolitan Police Service and is widely regarded as one of the founders of the Conservative Party. His third son, Captain William Peel, was one of the earliest to be awarded the Victoria Cross. He was also instrumental in building the railway

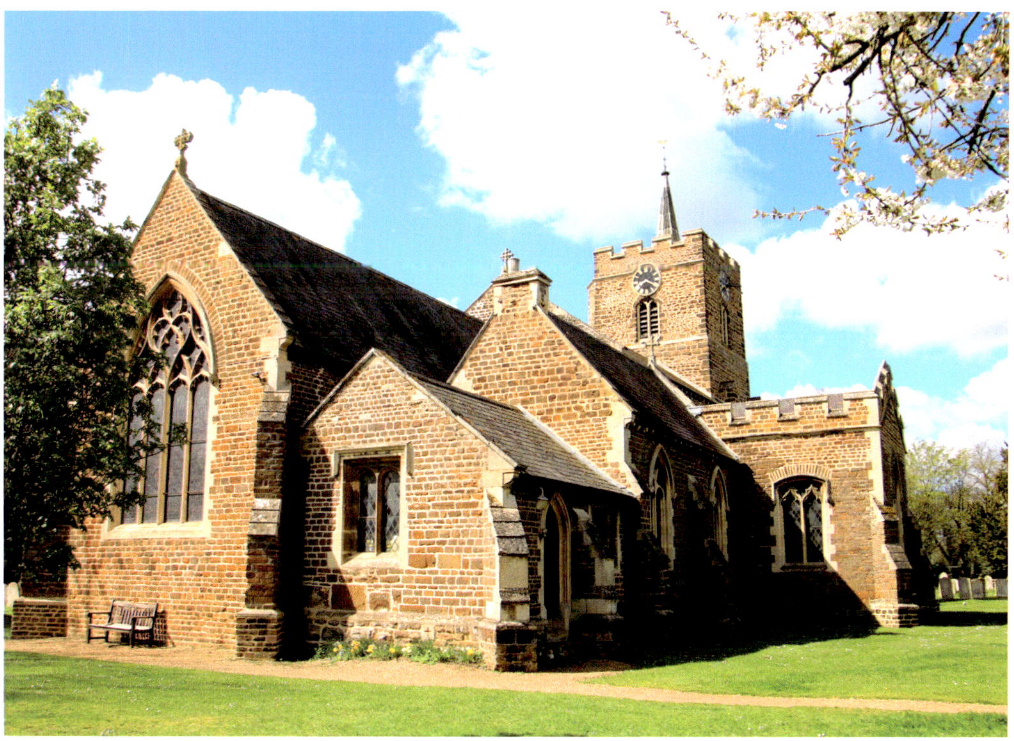

Sandy Church.

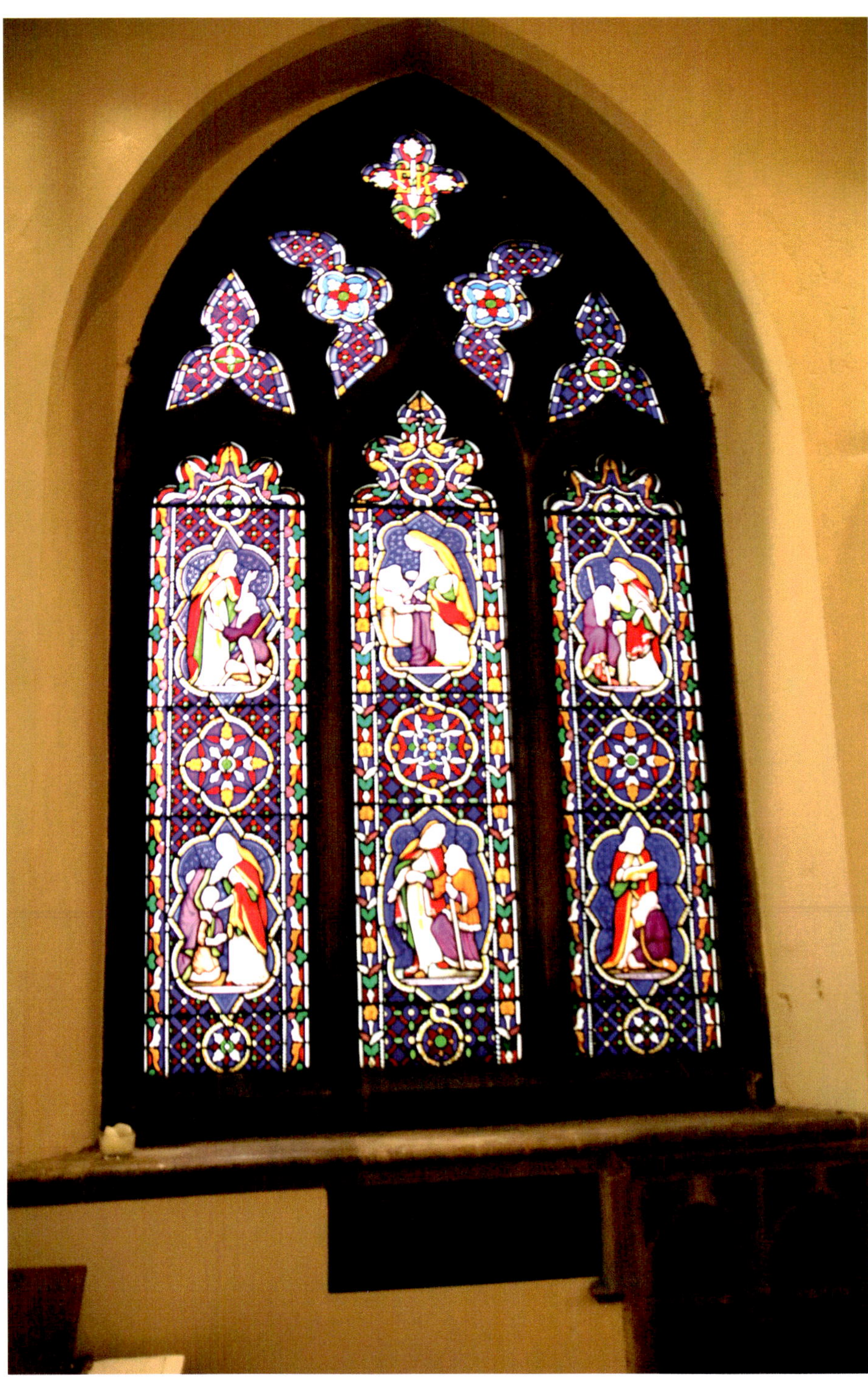

Window, Sandy.

from Sandy to Potton. The statue in his memory was placed in the chancel in 1861, later being moved to its present position in the south transept.

The Pym family also have a long association with the Sandy area, dating back to at least the mid-eighteenth century. They, like the Peels, were generous supporters of St Swithun's. The church contains a number of impressive family monuments and memorials. The Pyms had a family crypt at the church. Mysteriously, no entrance to this has been found. All that remains to be seen is a glass window in the floor of the north transept which has been bricked up from the underside and today is covered by a rug.

The former home of Captain William Peel is now the RSPB gatehouse and serves as the charity's visitor centre and gift shop. The visitor to Sandy is encouraged to take the Captain Peel Walk which commences at St Swithun's Church, to view his statue, and follows the disused Sandy and Potton Railway towards this gatehouse, on the Greensand Ridge.

The churchyard contains the tombs of Sir Frederick Liddell and his wife. Sir Frederick's sister is known to be the inspiration behind Lewis Carroll's *Alice in Wonderland*.

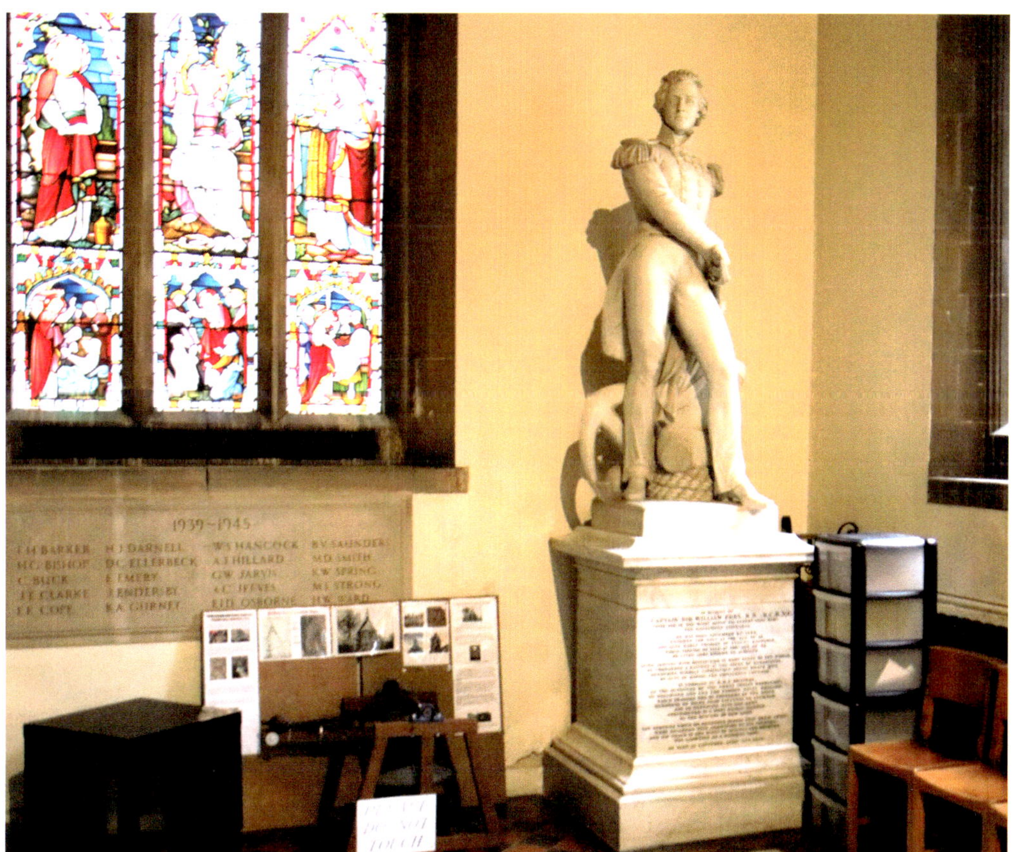

Captain William Peel memorial, Sandy.

THE CAPTAIN PEEL WALK, SANDY

An illustrated leaflet has been published detailing the route of this special Anniversary Walk.

The walk starts at Sandy Parish Church (to view Peel's statue) and then proceeds to the railway station (to recall the Sandy to Potton Railway). It continues along the Potton Road and enters The Lodge (RSPB) reserve at the bottom of the hill. It then passes through the restored heathland landscape to the RSPB Gatehouse (The Swiss Cottage – the former home of Captain Peel) and returns to Sandy via Stratford Road.

Walk from Sandy Church.

39. SHARNBROOK, ST PETER

The substantial village of Sharnbrook, with a population of over 2,000, lies 7 miles to the northwest of Bedford, just off the main A6 road and close to the River Great Ouse. The church of St Peter's sits in the middle of the village, on Church Lane, with its impressive octagonal spire resting on the fourteenth-century tower. This spire was added in the fifteenth century.

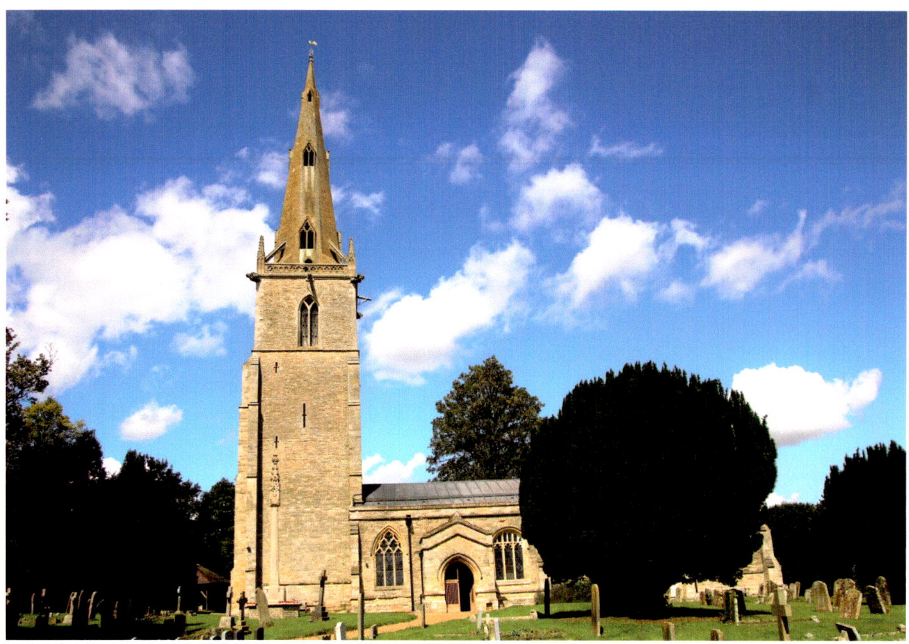

Sharnbrook Church.

The visitor to this church is drawn to the colourful garden to the right of the entrance porch. On closer inspection the plaque reads 'Sharnbrook Salute to Caring Memorial Garden'. It continues to say 'This Memorial Garden is designed as a Salute to the generosity of spirit for Caring and Sharing that was prompted by the Coronavirus pandemic of 2020 and enabled us to rediscover the true meaning and significance of Community. It is our tribute to all who care and share,

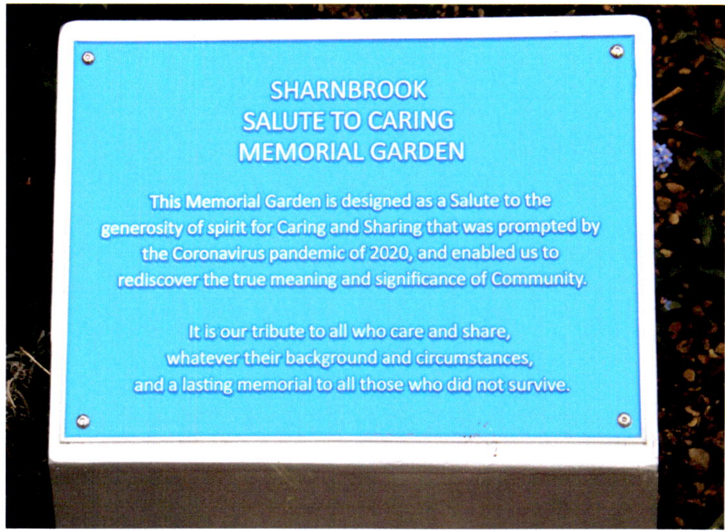

Right: Memorial garden, Sharnbrook.

Below: Memorial garden, Sharnbrook.

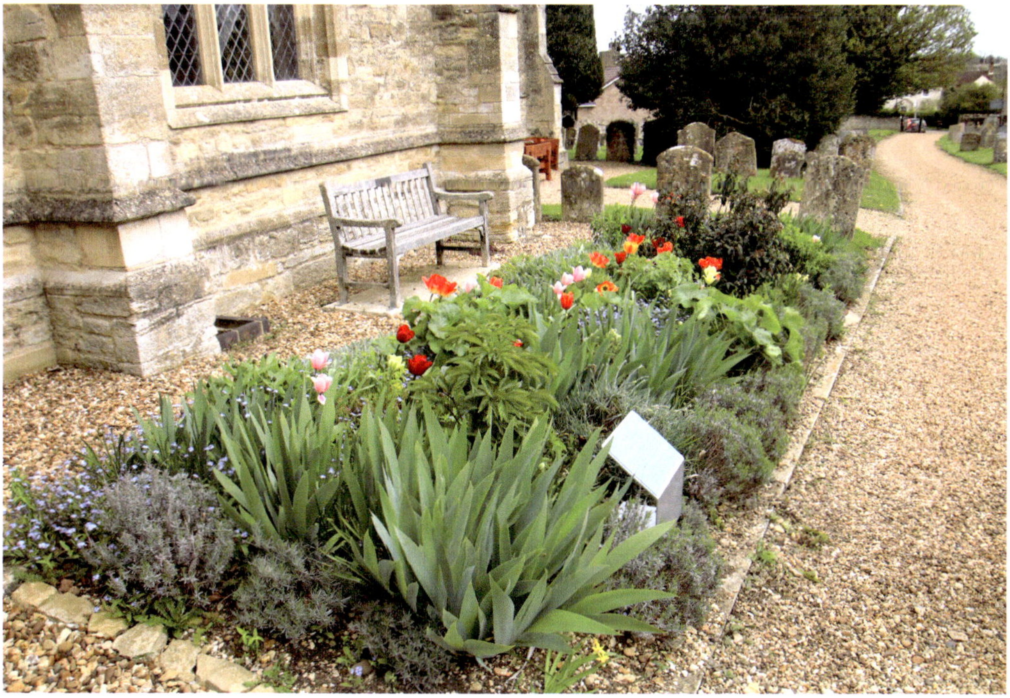

whatever their background and circumstances, and a lasting memorial to all those who did not survive.'

The oldest parts of the church, the aisles, date back to the thirteenth century. Within the church is the Tofte Chapel, named after Sir William Tofte, a member of the Knights Templar in the twelfth century. Sir William was gifted a manor house on land around half a mile away from the church. The manor passed through various families and was eventually purchased in 1876 by Charles Magniac.

The Tofte Chapel is today home to a Magniac family wall memorial. Hollingworth Magniac, who died in 1867, was a leading nineteenth-century merchant and connoisseur of medieval art. The churchyard contains a substantial rectangular family mausoleum. This stone monument was built in 1870 and designed by William Burgess inlaid with marble decoration. There are various inscriptions to members of the Magniac family.

St Peter's in Sharnbrook forms a benefice with St Mary's in Felmersham, All Saints in Souldrop and St Margaret of Antioch in Knotting.

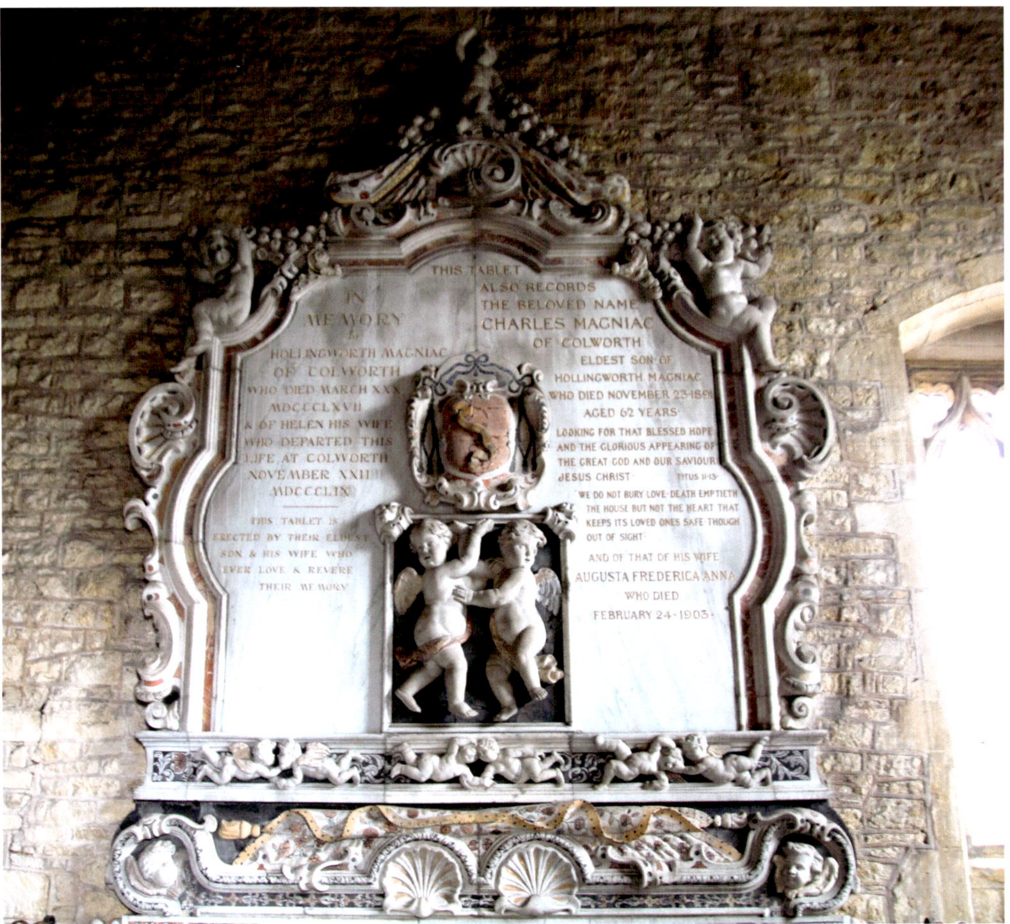

Magniac memorial, Sharnbrook.

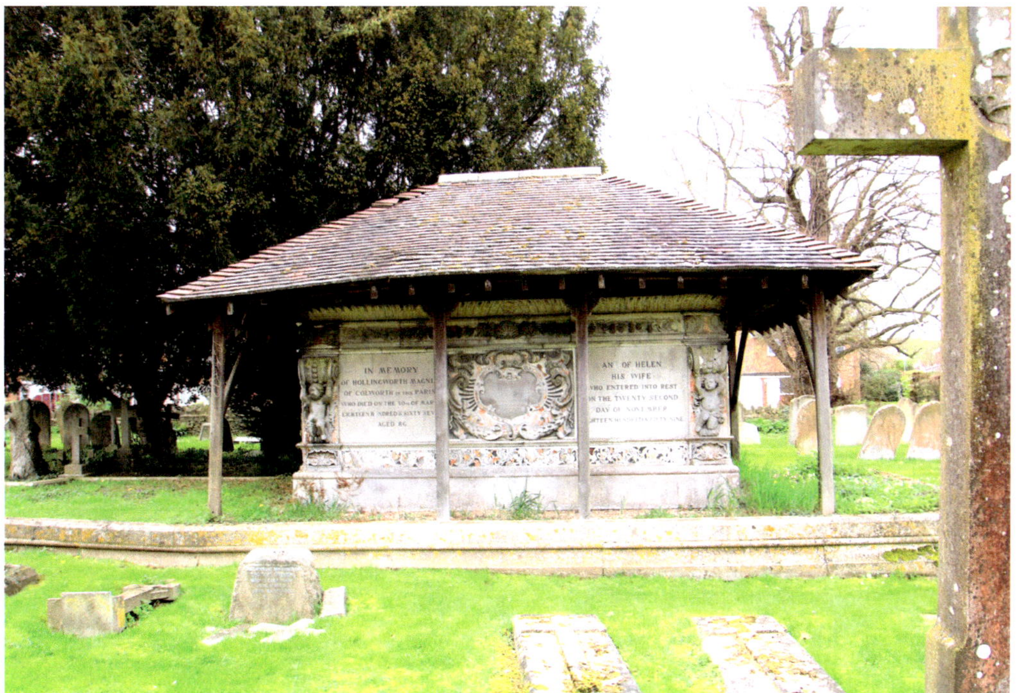

Magniac mausoleum, Sharnbrook.

40. SHILLINGTON, ALL SAINTS

The village of Shillington, with a population approaching 2,000, lies close to the Bedfordshire border with Hertfordshire. With the church's prominent position looking over the hills of the same name, it's easy to see why it is referred to as the 'Cathedral of the Chilterns'. This reference is accredited to none other than the Poet Laureate Sir John Betjeman. Perched on the top of a chalk hill, it is certainly a landmark visible for miles around.

The site has been a place of worship for over a thousand years. It was originally a Saxon church, replaced by a Norman one in the thirteenth century. This latter church was the subject of extensive ongoing rebuilding work, which, interrupted by the Black Death, was not completed until around 1370. The church as you see it now is little altered from this. Constant maintenance has been required, particularly in 1701 when a storm caused the tower to collapse. The rebuilding of the tower was not completed for half a century, whilst the considerable funds were raised by local residents and a wider appeal. All Saints Church is the parish church for Shillington which forms part of the benefice along with Gravenhurst and Stondon.

On entering the church, which pleasingly is open every day of the year, a warm welcome awaits you. The visitor is offered a great deal of information regarding the building itself, its bells together with local social history. There is also a ring-bound book which you are encouraged to take around with you to help

                 Churches of Bedfordshire

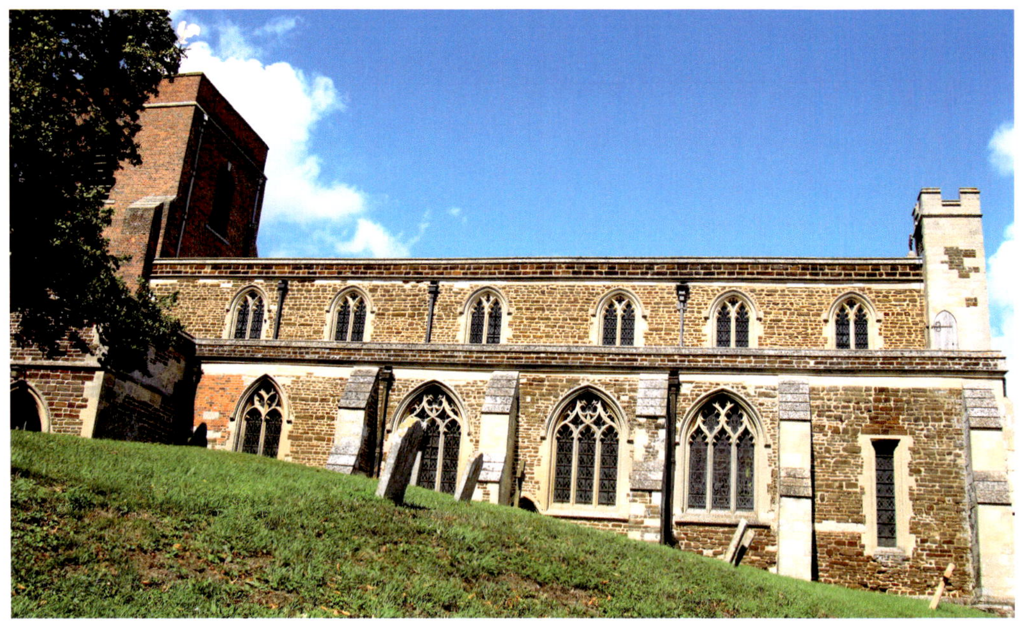

Shillington Church.

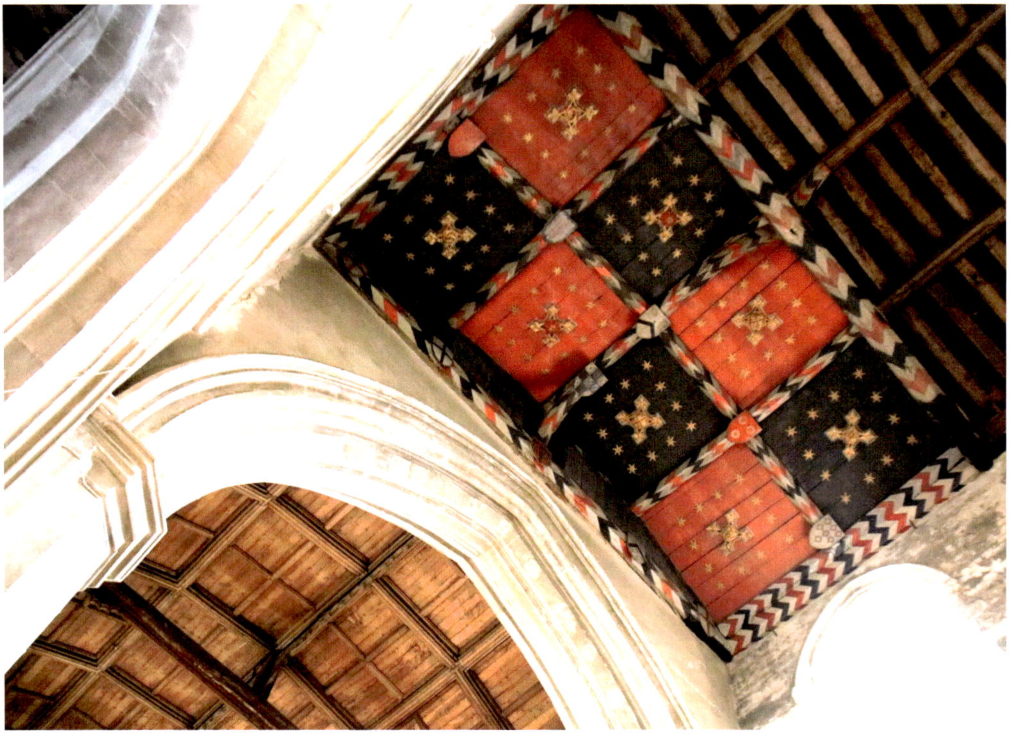

Roof, Shillington Church.

you identify specific features within the building. On stepping down the nave, the eye is drawn to the colourful roof which was almost certainly painted during the Middle Ages. Information in the church states its last major renovation was in 1746.

The present church was completed under the guidance of Matthew Asscheton, whose sense of humour was conveyed by the inclusion of two small stone carvings. An 'ass' and a 'barrel – or 'tun', an obvious pun on his name, are evidently to be found on the building's west end exterior!

Another quirky aspect of this building's history is 'Postgate's Folly'. No one knows what Revd L. H. Postgate had in mind when, in 1921, he designed and built this pulpit. Outside the church, you can view this folly as it gives an external entry to the vestry.

The church's beauty can be admired after dark from miles around. This is thanks to the church's participation in the Millennium church floodlighting project back in 1999/2000. All Saints has continued this practice to this day. The church is illuminated every night from dusk to around midnight. Sponsorship of this lighting is available to all parishioners as a poignant commemoration to their lost friends and loved ones.

41. SOULDROP, ALL SAINTS

This north Bedfordshire village lies close to the county boundary with Northamptonshire. Souldrop, together with the smaller community of Knotting, was incorporated into the parish of 'Knotting with Souldrop' in 1934, and today the two villages have a combined population of around 250. The benefice consists of Sharnbrook, Felmersham, and Knotting with Souldrop.

The church of All Saints is accessed by a footpath off the Sharnbrook road to the southeast of the village. There has, in fact, been a church on this Souldrop site since 1270, with the spire being one of the oldest in the county of Bedfordshire. This spire has been retained, whilst the majority of the building was replaced in 1800 and, then again, in 1860 following a serious fire. This Victorian era rebuild was overseen by architect Henry Clutton, a particular favourite of the Duke of Bedford, from nearby Souldrop Manor.

The ornate spire is octagonal and topped with a weathercock. The south porch has a steep pitch tiled roof to match the other roofs of the church. The north transept has a large rose window with six petals, with a gable cross on top of its pitch.

The tiny community of Knotting is located at the extreme north of the county of Bedfordshire. Once serving the nearby manor, now long gone, St Margaret of Antioch's Church can best be described today as a village church unspoilt by modern day. Indeed, on visiting we felt as if we had stepped into a time warp. It is now in the hands of The Churches Conservation Trust, with its last regular service in 2007 and a thanksgiving one-off a few years later after restoration.

Knotting's place in social history dates back almost 400 years previous. In 1637, it came to light that on three consecutive Shrove Tuesdays from 1634, the chancel had been used for cock-fighting and associated betting by not just the parishioners,

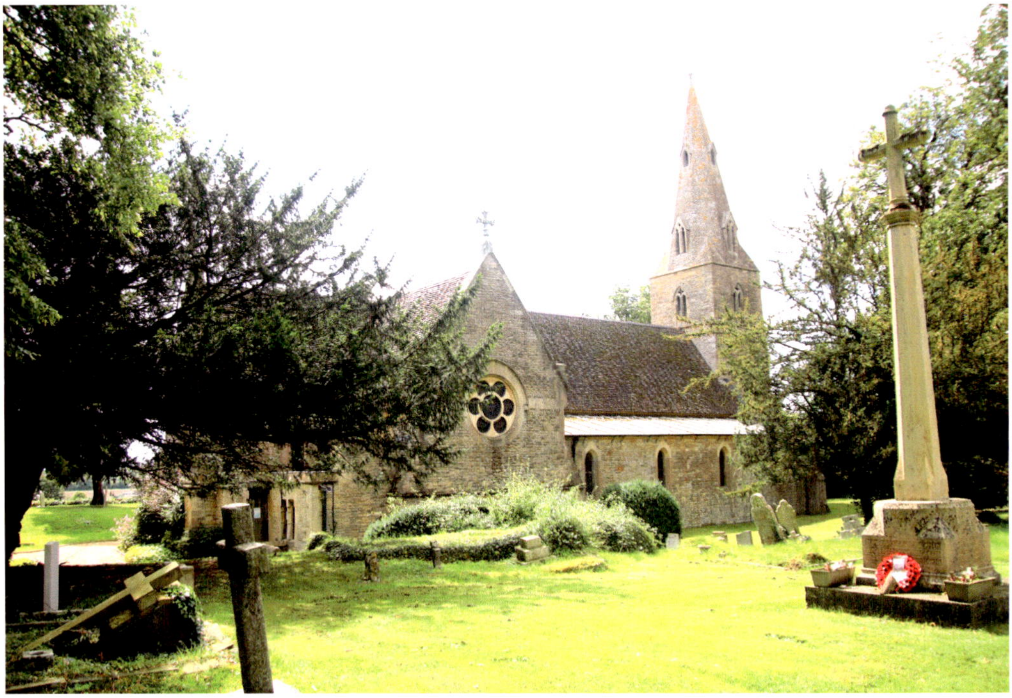

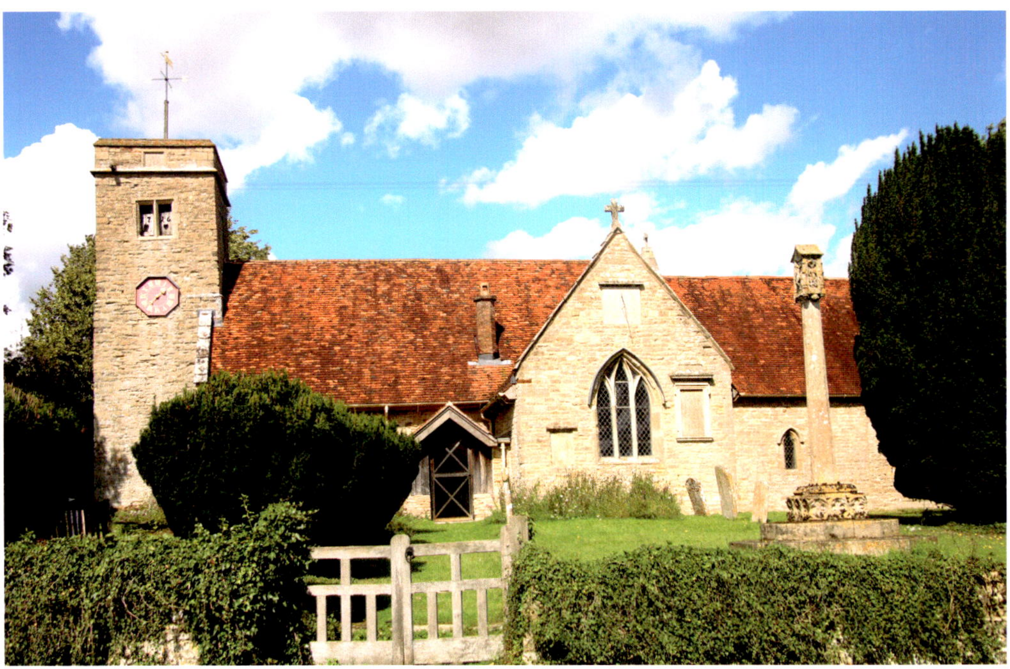

Souldrop Church.

Knotting Church.

but the rector and churchwardens. As a result, on the order of Archbishop Laud, spiked gates were erected below the chancel arch to prevent any reoccurrence and the rector was subsequently defrocked.

42. STEVINGTON, ST MARY

The parish of Stevington lies on the River Great Ouse around 5 miles northwest of Bedford. The village has a population of just over 500. It is in the Chellington team ministry, which consists of a total of eight churches. Stevington is joined with St Mary's, Carlton; St Peter's, Harrold; All Saints, Odell; St Mary the Virgin, Podington with Farndish; St Lawrence, Wymington; All Saint's, Turvey; along with the United Reformed Church, Harrold.

The visitor to the village may have been drawn by its impressive windmill, a well-known local landmark. The church of St Mary the Virgin itself can be found in the north of the village overlooking the river. It exudes an air of tranquillity, boasting a variety of hedgerow wildlife and plants.

The church is built on the site of a well, which is located at the east end of the church wall, in an arched recess. Just follow the 'Bunyan Trail' footpath, signposted from the church gate. This is one of only two wells regarded as 'holy' in the county of Bedfordshire. Pilgrims were regular visitors in the hope of its waters curing eye ailments. Locals claim that it has neither run dry or frozen over. The area is a habitat for the butterbur plant, historically known as a treatment for coughs, asthma and hay fever amongst many others.

The church itself dates back to the 1280s, with completion around a century later. Some restoration has taken place in the nineteenth century.

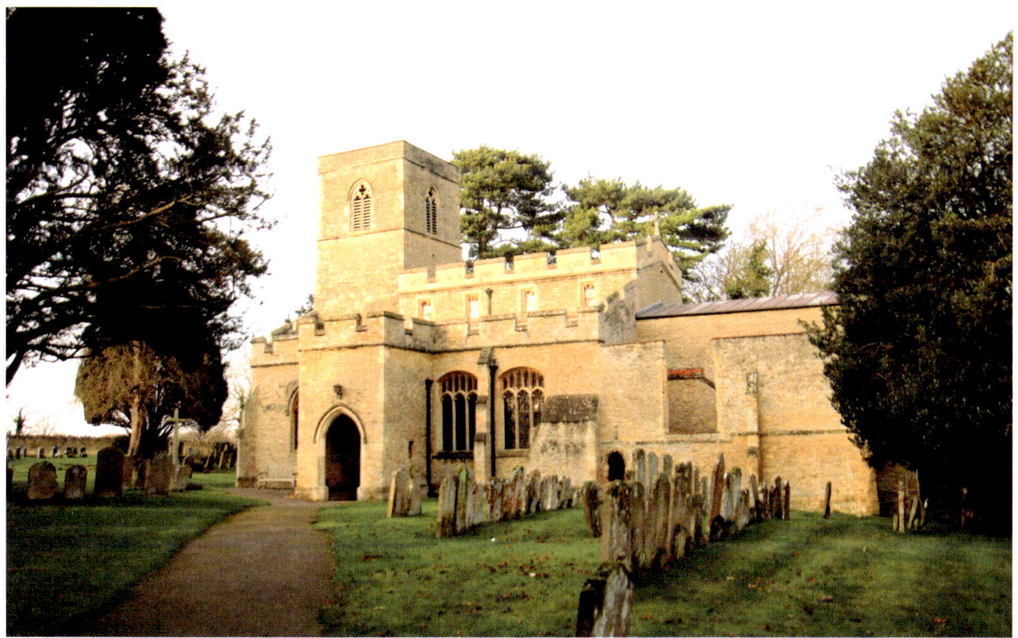

Stevington Church.

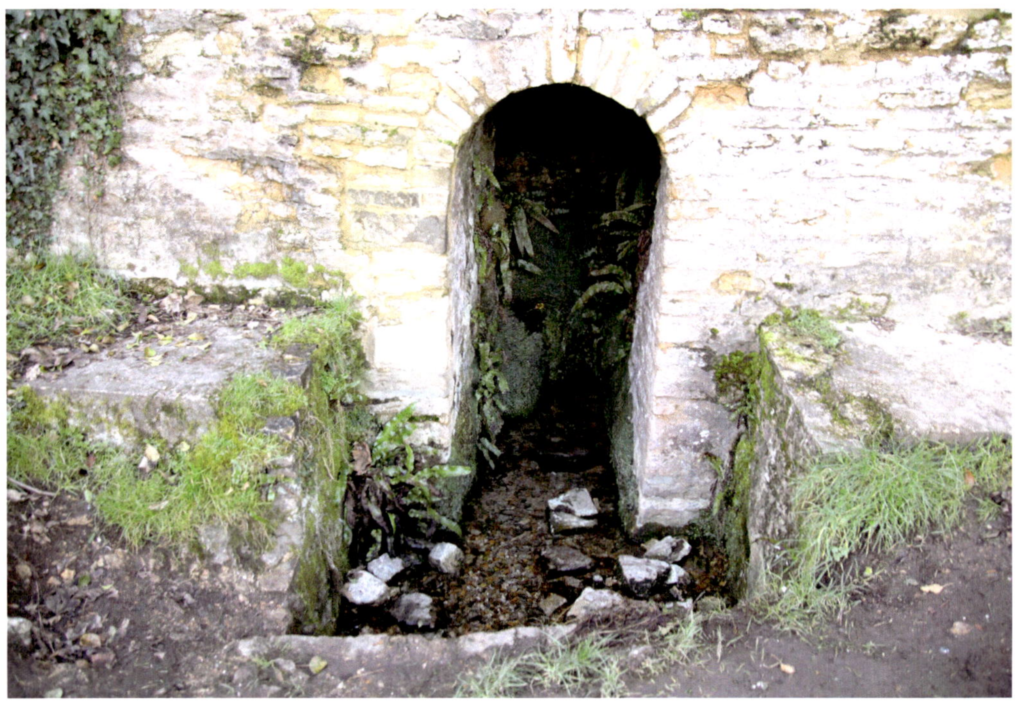

'Holy well', Stevington.

43. Stotfold, St Mary the Virgin

Stotfold is a growing town in Bedfordshire, 15 miles southeast of Bedford, close to the Hertfordshire border. The River Ivel passes through the town, which has a population of around 12,000. The oldest surviving building in the town is St Mary's parish church, situated to the east and accessed via a track from Church Road.

The present church, which dates from 1150, is probably on the site of a former wooden Saxon church. Evidence of this was found in 1890 when work in the nave led to the excavation of a Saxon coffin containing bones dating back prior to the present church building.

The church was built of flint with Ashwell clunch and was originally a church with just a nave and chancel, and no aisles. It has evolved over time into its present structure. In 1320, a north aisle was added, and in 1370 the south aisle was extended to its present size. Evidence of its original outer facing can be seen on the two internal pillars which were left as supports. The tower was added in 1450 and the chancel was widened. In 1480, lead was used to replace the originally thatched nave roof.

The tower was restored in 1927. It appears in contrast to the rest of the church as it has a rendered finish. During more recent repairs to the tower and its roof, graffiti was discovered. This dates back to 1860, although some may be older, and up to 1900. Some of this graffiti can be linked to several Stotfold families of that era.

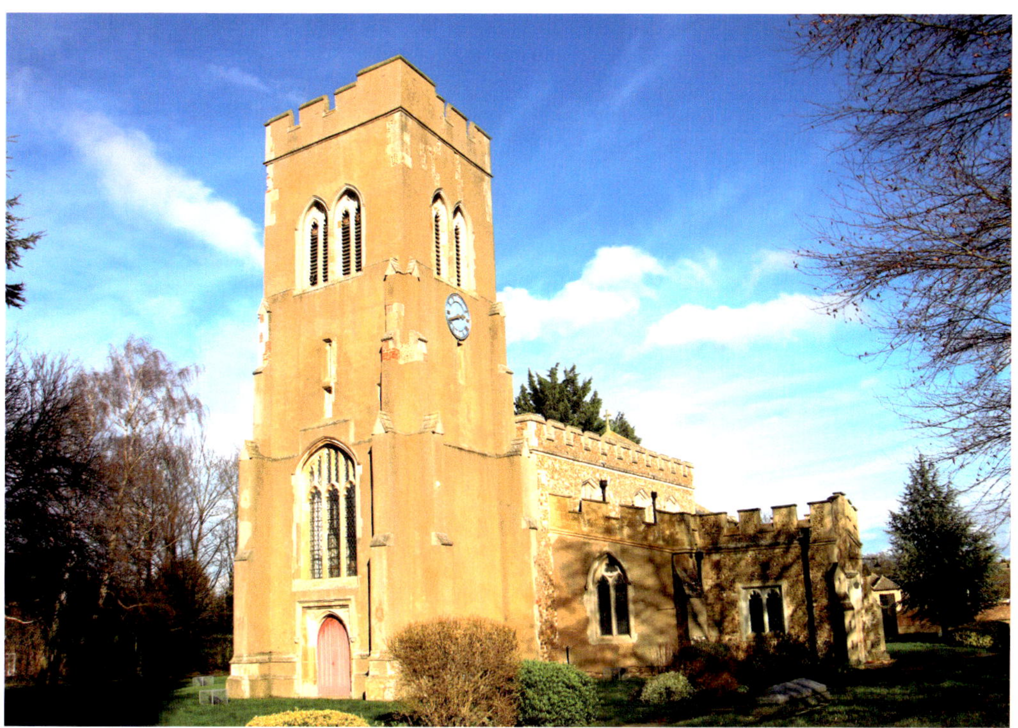

Stotfold Church.

The tower originally housed five bells, two of which were sold. Today, eight bells proudly inhabit a metal frame. In 1948, three new bells were fitted in memory of Stotfold's Second World War heroes. The remaining three original bells were also recast at this time. In 1976, local ringers added two additional bells, one of which was a treble. All the bells have been tuned to the 1484 eldest bell. St Mary's has every right to be proud of its bellringing history.

On entering the church, one's eyes are drawn to its wooden screen. It also has a 1920 memorial stained-glass window of St George and St Michael. This is in memory of those who lost their lives in the First World War. It's octagonal font dates from the fourteenth century.

St Mary's Church forms a benefice with Radwell church (in Hertfordshire).

44. STUDHAM, ST MARY

The Chiltern village of Studham lies to the southwest of the county, close to the borders of both Buckinghamshire and Hertfordshire, in an area of outstanding natural beauty. Its population is around 1,100.

The church of St Mary the Virgin was difficult to find amongst the narrow, leafy lanes of the village. Its bland, cemented exterior gives it an appearance unlike the majority of churches in Bedfordshire. With evidence of a church being here since before the Norman Conquest, the earliest part of today's building dates from the thirteenth century.

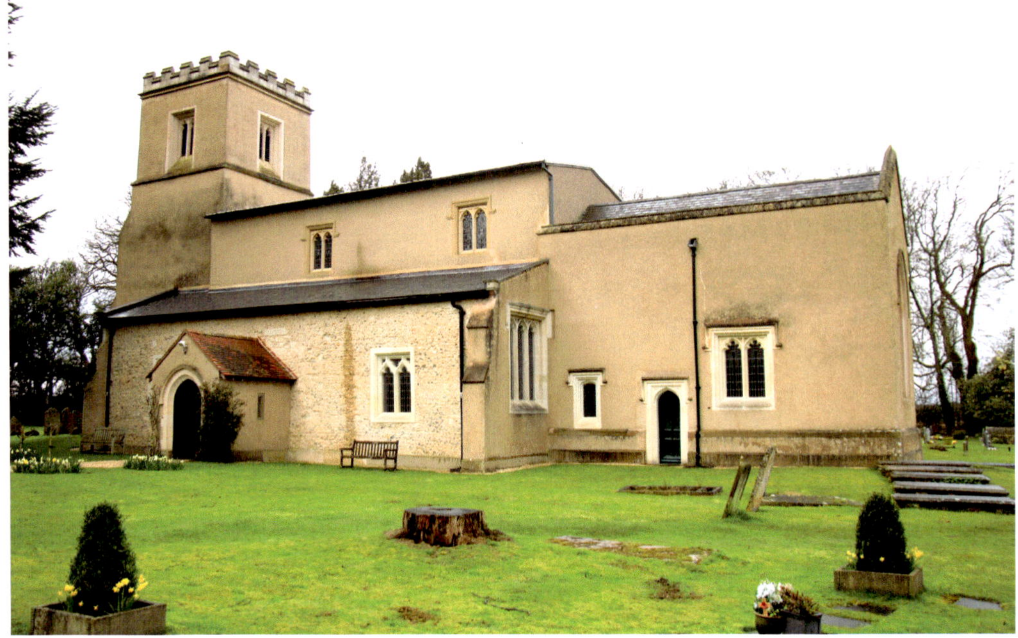

Studham Church.

On entering the church, the visitor's eye is drawn to the distinctively unusual pulpit. It is made of Cornish serpentine granite and was installed in memory of Revd Charles Wagstaffe. Wagstaffe was a long-serving vicar in the second half of the nineteenth century.

The church's font is likely to date from Norman times, with the flowing dragon carvings on its bowl being particularly unusual. A hand-drawn outline diagram of the church's interior states that 'the Norman font predates the church, only one other like it in Chichester'.

In 1982, the United Benefice of Kensworth, Studham and Whipsnade was formed. By contrast to the exterior of Studham church, the Church of St Mary the Virgin in nearby Kensworth is appeasing to the eye. It greets you with its distinctively patterned slate roof on the south side of the nave. The majority of the remainder of the church *is* built of flint and the tower from differing materials including local Totternhoe limestone. Although once at its heart, today the church is situated to the north of the main village. It dates from the twelfth century. Once inside, the font captures the visitor's attention. Said to be as old as the church itself, this plain artefact is impressive by its very size, suggesting its use in the days when babies were baptised by total immersion.

Whipsnade village is, of course, well renowned for its world-famous zoo. The church of St Mary Magdalene in Whipsnade is set back from the village green, often unnoticed by the zoo's many visitors who pass by. There has been a place of worship on the site since Anglo-Saxon times, but the present building was started as recently as the late sixteenth century. The oldest part is the tower, dating from

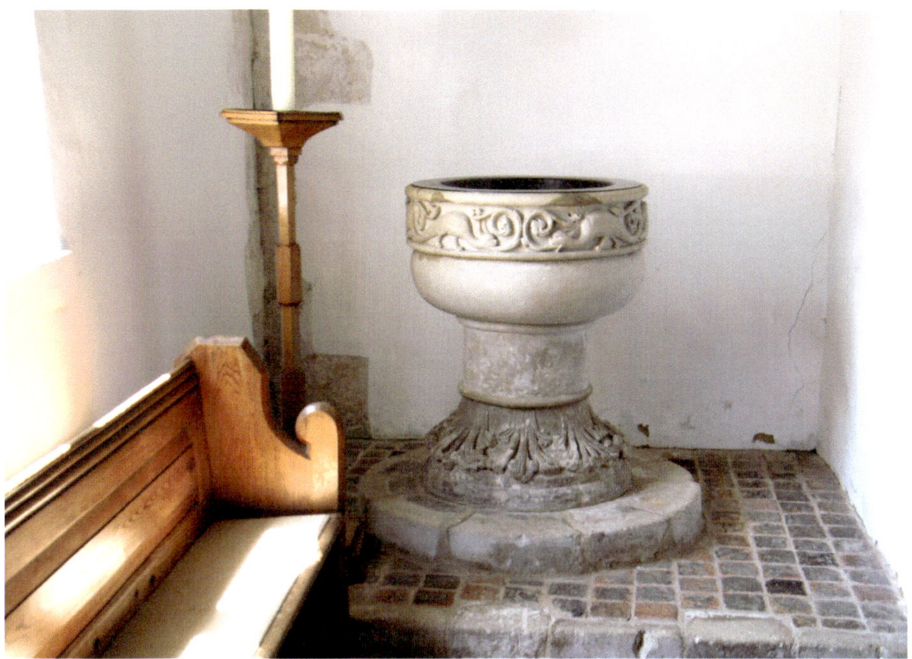

Font, Studham.

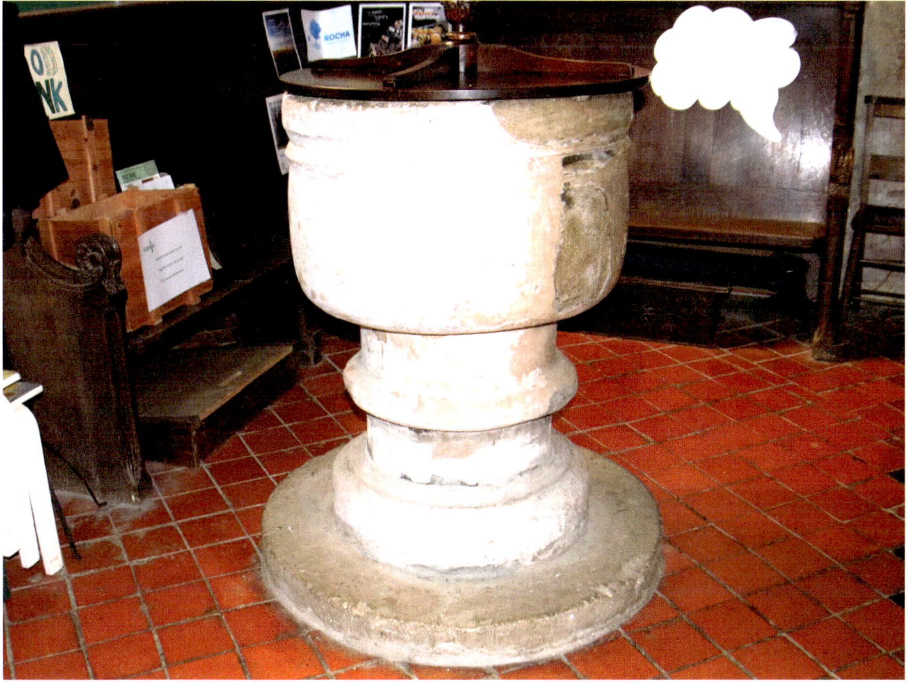

Font, Kensworth Church.

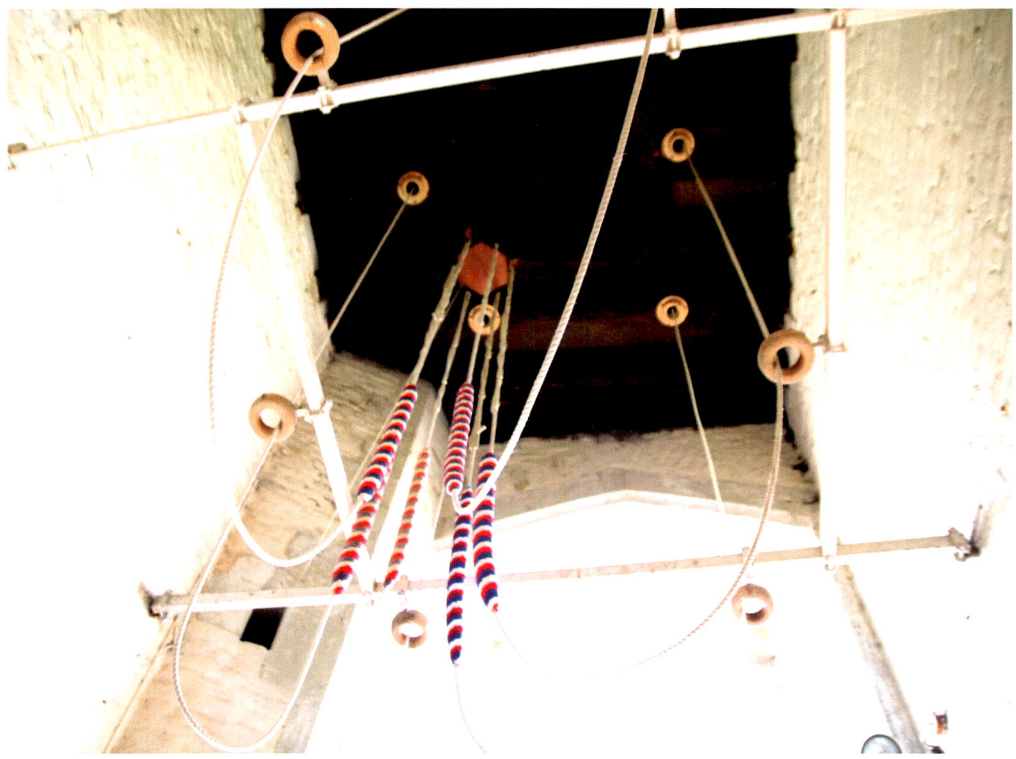

Bell ropes, Whipsnade.

1590, constructed of some of the earliest examples of locally produced and fired clay brickwork.

Despite the small community it serves, the church at Whipsnade has been extremely well maintained, with new facilities tastefully incorporated into the building. It enjoys an active team of bellringers, with the ropes of the church bells on proud display beneath the tower at the church's rear.

45. TEMPSFORD, ST PETER

Tempsford lies on what was once the Great North Road, which has been superseded by the A1, where the rivers Ouse and Ivel meet. The village is split by the A1 and lies 7 miles from Bedford and 2 miles to the north of Sandy. It has a population of around 600.

St Peter's Church is situated on the west side of the village, nearer to Bedford, whereas the main part of the village lies to the east of the A1. Many church sites can be dated back to the twelfth century, however there is no evidence of this on the present-day site. The church of today dates from the fourteenth century with extensive rebuilding, extending and renovation work taking place in the seventeenth century.

Today, the seventeenth-century work is a delightful, distinctive feature of the church. The alternating rows of clunch and ironstone have produced coloured

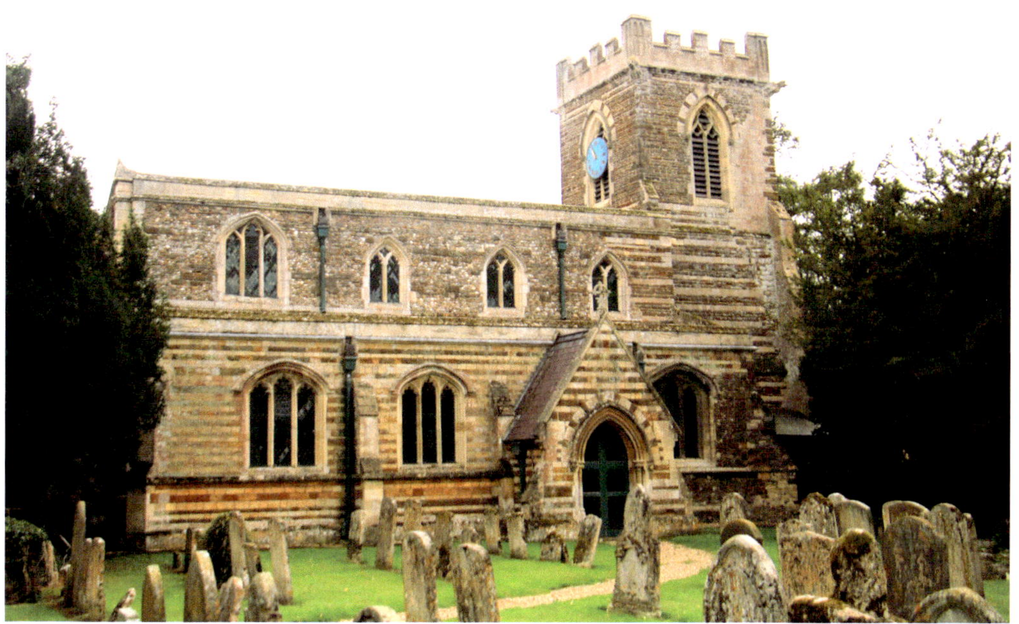

Tempsford Church.

banding around the church. The embattled tower, restored in the nineteenth century, is in three stages. It does, however, seem so low that the monsters on the top corners look remarkably realistic. One enters the church through the south porch. A similar entrance is on the north side; the door is, however, much lower. The church itself is rather plain with four bay pointed-arched arcades on either side.

The church has an allegiance to war veterans. It is close to a secret Second World War airfield where allied agents used to depart from to parachute into Europe. St Peter's east end of the north aisle is given over to remembrance. There is a window which was erected as a war memorial in 1920 and an oak memorial board with the names of fifteen 'men of Tempsford who nobly gave their lives for King and Country in the Great War of 1914 – 1919'.

The church is part of the Riversmeet benefice which includes All Saints, Great Barford; St Mary Magdelene, Roxton; St Denys, Little Barford; and St Edmund or St James, Blunham.

46. TOTTERNHOE, ST GILES

Totternhoe is situated in the southwest of Bedfordshire close to Leighton Buzzard and around 2 miles away from Dunstable. It is a long, thin village with a population of approximately 1,200. The church of St Giles is in the southeast of the village on the road leading to Eaton Bray and Edlesborough, close to the Buckinghamshire border.

There is a record of a church being on the site since the twelfth century. Work on the building we see today started in the fourteenth century and was not completed until the sixteenth century. Not surprisingly, the church is built predominantly from Totternhoe stone (clunch), mined from quarries only around a mile away.

The church is almost completely embattled and it also has five pinnacles above the aisles and four over the nave on each side. The south porch adds to the aesthetics of the church's exterior. It dates from the fifteenth century. Pictures of the church in 1812 show that the porch had a tiled roof. In 1833 a lot of repairs took place. This work seemed to include the restoration of the pinnacles, the alterations to the south porch, remodelling the chancel and the adding of the embattled parapets. The porch is dominated by its embattlement which is lower than the embattled south aisle chancel wall, which is clearly wider than the nave.

The east end of the church has a chequerboard pattern. This is a common feature on churches in this particular area. The effect is created by the use of flint alternating with Totternhoe clunch.

Further work took place in the early twentieth century with new stained-glass windows, choir stalls, organ and repairs to the tower and bell-frame which had been damaged in a fire in 1923. In 1953, two more bells were added to make a total of eight. Today the church is proud of its bellringing. A new ringing platform was built in the tower in 1967. Some of the bells date back to 1654.

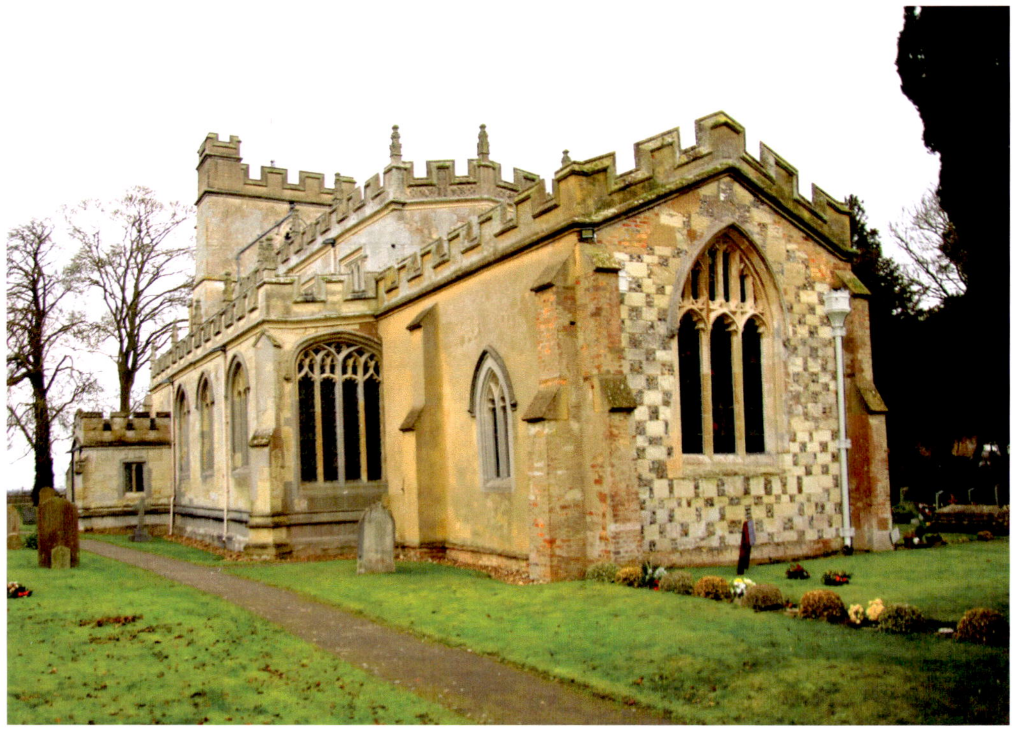

Totternhoe Church.

The churchyard is wonderfully maintained, encouraging natural visitors as well as parishioners. It is home to birdboxes, hedgehog houses, log piles for insects, bird feeders and a fenced pond to encourage aquatic creatures. This is all maintained by dedicated churchgoers.

St Giles of Totternhoe is in a benefice with St John the Baptist Church at Stanbridge and All Saints Church at Tilsworth.

47. TURVEY, ALL SAINTS

The village of Turvey sits on the east bank of the River Great Ouse. It is 7 miles west of Bedford, close to the Buckinghamshire border. The village is on the A428 linking Bedford to Northampton and has a population of around 1,000.

All Saints Church is situated in the centre of the village on the northern side of the main road. It is a large church with the oldest parts dating back to Saxon times. Like so many of the Bedfordshire churches, it has a layered, embattled exterior and tower with a small spire topped with its cross.

One enters the churchyard via a beautiful lychgate. This was originally constructed in 1856 and restored in 1925. The thirteenth-century porch with its fifteenth-century embattled top is the main entrance. The interior portrays its evolution through historical times. In the southwest corner of the nave, two late Saxon windows remain. The font has an unusual four-cornered design and dates from the early 1200s.

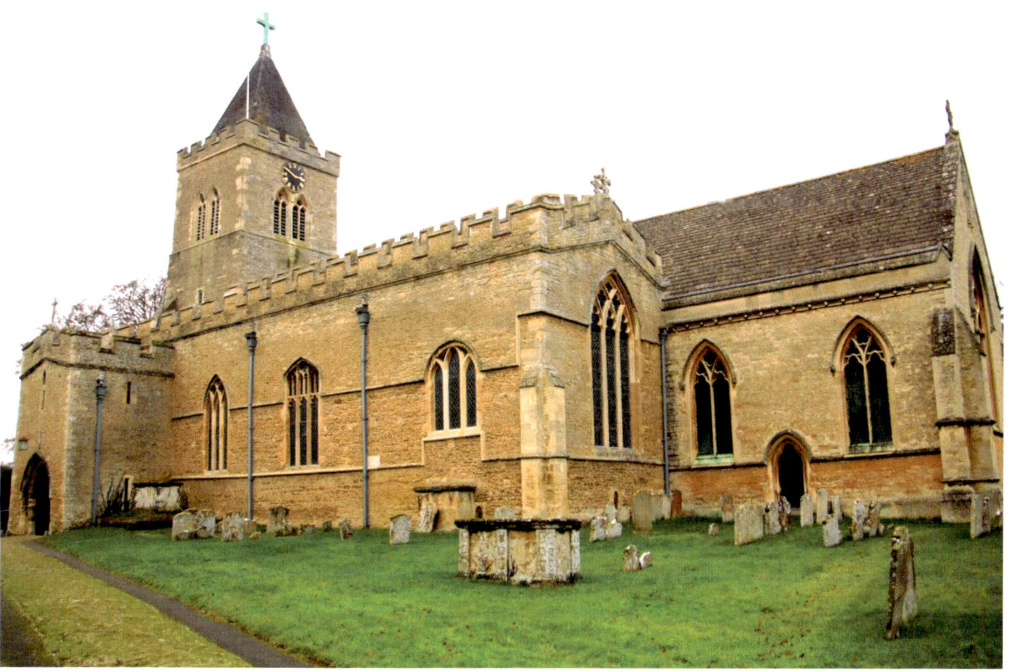

Turvey Church.

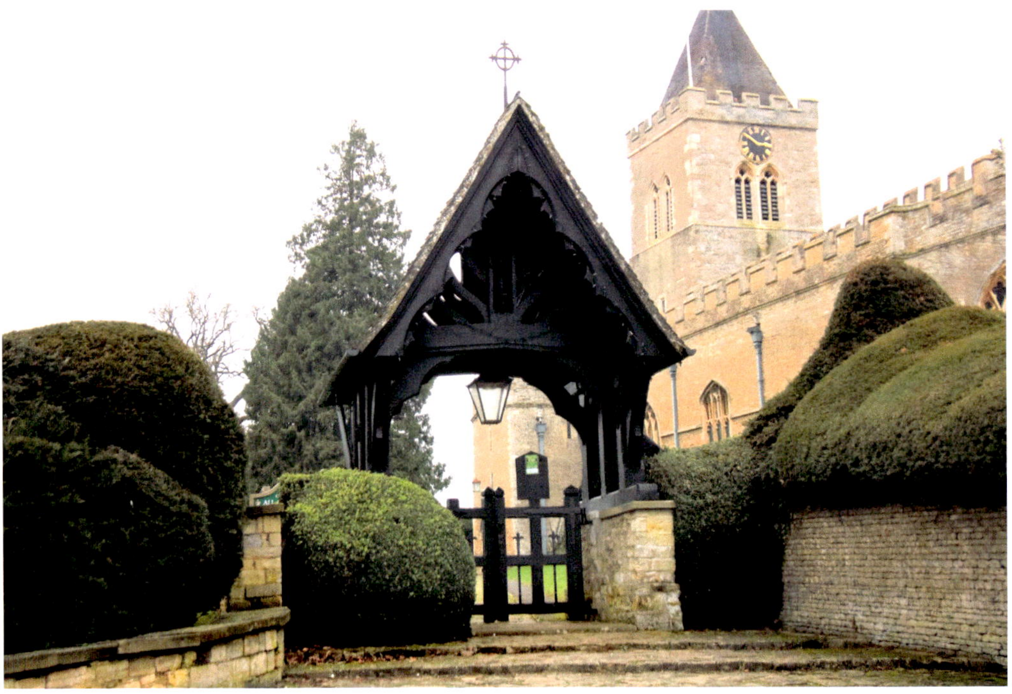

Lychgate, Turvey.

The church is perhaps best known for its brasswork and elaborate tomb memorials to members of the Mordaunt family. Turvey village was owned by this family until the eighteenth century. There is a 1506 tomb of Sir John Mordaunt and his wife. He was appointed as 'King's Sergeant' by Henry VII. There is also a large tomb to the first Lord Mordaunt and his wife. He was High Sheriff of Bedfordshire and Buckinghamshire in 1509 and 1510. Henry VIII made him Baron Mordaunt in 1532. The tomb of the second Lord Mordaunt and his two wives is probably the most unusual. This is due to his effigy being on a higher level than that of his wives. There is also a simple memorial tomb to Lewis, the third Lord Mordaunt, which has a marble and black alabaster top. He is better known as the 'reluctant' judge at the trial of Mary, Queen of Scots.

The Mordaunt family sold the estate in 1786 to the Higgins family. In later years, history has them recorded as two family branches, the Higgins and the Longuet Higgins. They were responsible for much of the restorative and rebuilding work. The churchyard has a large mausoleum for the Longuet Higgins family.

The church forms part of the large Chellington group of churches.

48. Willington, St Lawrence

The village of Willington lies around 5 miles to the east of the county town of Bedford. Willington has a population today of around 800. The church of St Lawrence is situated to the west of the village, close to the National Trust properties of Willington Dovecote and Stables.

With mention in the Domesday Book, it is thought there has been a place of worship in the village since before the Norman Conquest in 1066. The Gostwick family had a centuries old connection with the village. In 1529, John Gostwick served both Cardinal Wolsey and Henry VIII and purchased the parish of Willington. In so doing, he became Lord of the Manor. In the 1540s, he was responsible for the building of both the Dovecote and Stables, as well as rebuilding St Lawrence's Church.

Sir John Gostwick was knighted by Henry VIII in 1541. Today, the north chapel is known as the Gostwick chapel, and it is here that we find the monuments to the family.

Much later, the church was served by Revd Augustus Orlebar, who was the vicar for more than fifty years until his death at the local vicarage in 1912. A plaque is displayed on the wall of the chancel to both him and his wife. He oversaw many improvements to the church during this period. This work included a new font, alterations to both the pulpit and pews as well as overseeing a locally built organ being installed in 1875. The distinctive tiles in the chancel and sanctuary were laid around this time, said to be replicas of fourteenth-century tiles found in the church during this restoration. As a footnote, the nineteenth-century organ has subsequently been replaced.

St Lawrence's Church had to overcome a much more modern challenge earlier this century. The local bat population of both brown long-eared and pipistrelle

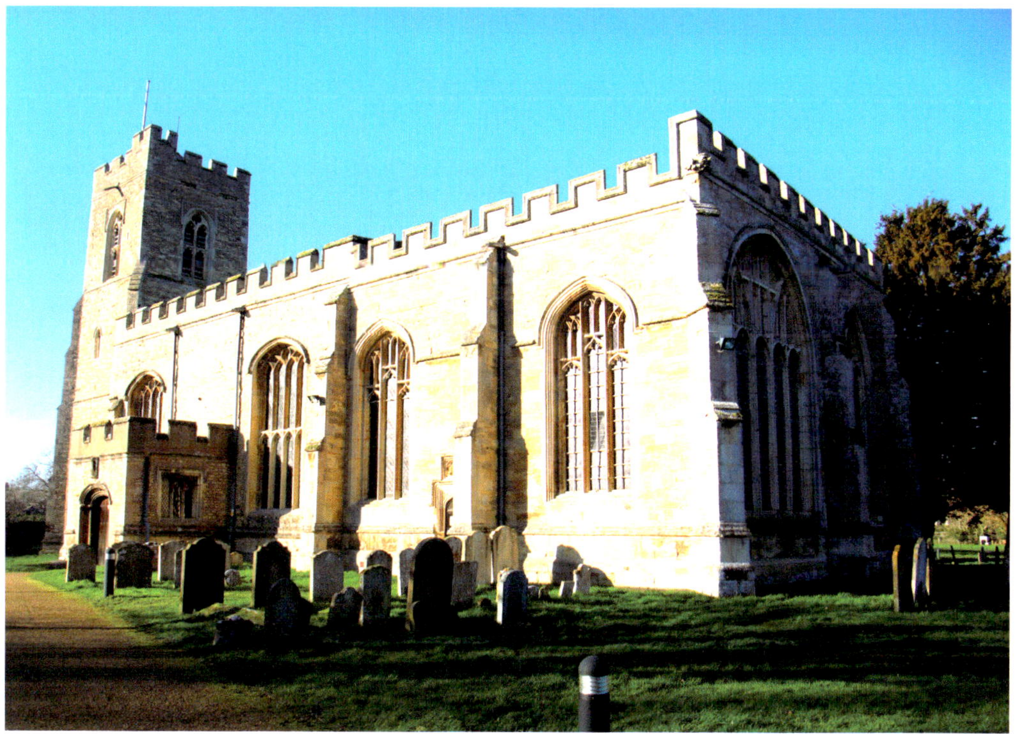

Willington Church.

species took to roosting throughout the church. This resulted in considerable cleaning taking place before a revolutionary heated bat box was installed in 2020. This was disguised as a hatchment covering the bats' entry into the building, overcoming the problem.

St Lawrence Church in Willington is part of a three-church benefice, together with All Saints, Cople and St John the Evangelist, Moggerhanger.

49. WOBURN, ST MARY

The village of Woburn lies around 5 miles south of the city of Milton Keynes, close to the M1 motorway. It has a population of around 1,000, with a further 2,000 people living in the adjacent community of Woburn Sands. The latter, including the parish church of St Michael's, straddles the county boundary of Bedfordshire and Buckinghamshire. Woburn is known in the wider community as the home of a wildlife park and abbey, the latter being the seat of the Dukes of Bedford. The quaint village of Woburn lies on the edge of the estate, including the remains of the ancient medieval church to be found on Bedford Street.

In 1864, most of the church was demolished, leaving just the original tower. The site was, however, deemed unsuitable for the planned rebuilding of St Mary's and a new site needed to be found. The former church was rebuilt as a mortuary chapel and today serves as Woburn Heritage Centre.

The replacement church was built on nearby Park Street later in the 1860s by Henry Clutton, an architect who had studied French medieval building styles. This

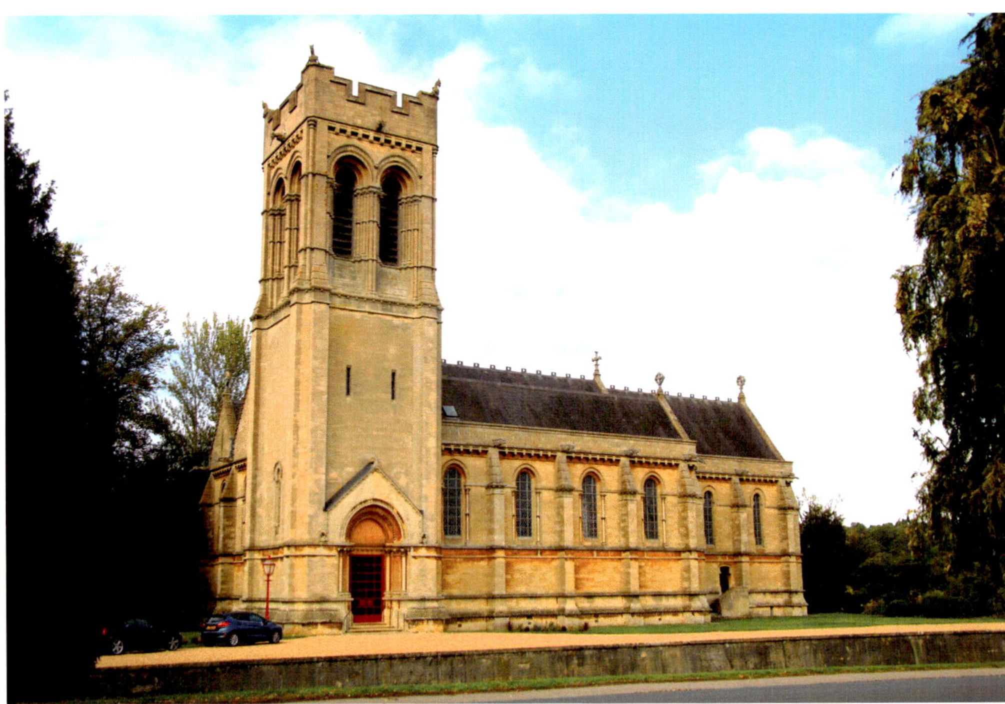

Woburn Church.

explains why the 'new' church at Woburn is typical of a French Gothic cathedral. This work originally included a tall spire, nearly 200 feet high and a county landmark at the time, but was dismantled in 1890 on safety grounds.

The noble building was constructed for William Russell, 8th Duke of Bedford, with the large crypt originally intended as a resting place for members of the Duke's family. It has, however, not been used for this purpose and was subsequently redesigned as a well-equipped function room, popular today for weddings and other family occasions. A recent example of this occurred in May 2015 when St Mary's Church hosted the wedding of Spice Girl Geri Halliwell to Christian Horner, the former Formula One driver.

An impressive stained-glass window at the eastern end of the south aisle depicts St Francis of Assisi standing amongst the birds and flowers, presumably of the Woburn Abbey estate. This window commemorates the life of the Duchess Mary Russell, wife of the 11th Duke of Bedford. The inscription reads 'Whose work was in the hospitals, whose delight was in the birds'. This summarises her mission in life to care for the sick and injured, including the building and running of Maryland cottage hospital in Woburn, treating wounded soldiers during the First World War. The window and inscription reflect her lifelong love for ornithology.

She later became known as 'The Flying Duchess'. This familiar nickname was due to her love of birds and, later, aviation. She took to the skies at the age of sixty, making record-breaking flights to Cape Town and Karachi. She met her death in March 1937, at the age of seventy-one, her plane leaving Woburn only to crash in the North Sea. Her body was never recovered.

St Mary's Church, in Woburn, forms a benefice with St Peter's, Milton Bryan; St Peter and All Saints, Battlesden; St Mary's, Potsgrove; and St John the Baptist, Eversholt.

50. WOOTTON, ST MARY

The village of Wootton lies to the southwest of the county town of Bedford. It is relatively low lying, close to the River Great Ouse within Bedford's Clay Vale. Its mention in the Domesday Book claims a population of twenty-six, made up of twenty villagers and six slaves. Today, its population has grown to around 4,000 as a result of Bedford and Kempston's urban development.

The present church of St Mary's is situated to the southwest of the village at the junction of Church Road and Hall End Road. It dates back to the fourteenth century, although local records reveal a vicar of Wootton as far back as 1251. It is likely there was a place of worship on the site since before the Norman Conquest.

On entering the church, the height of the arcades can't fail to impress. There is much evidence of the church restoration work carried out over the years, with a new organ and font both added in the 1850s. At the time the Revd Frederick Neale was the vicar, with his sister providing the funds for the organ. The octagonal font has a highly decorative wooden cover which catches the eye of visitors. The Neales were also responsible for many other alterations and additions within the church. These include a new pulpit and restoration work to the north porch. He also installed elaborate candelabras, the chains of which remain in existence.

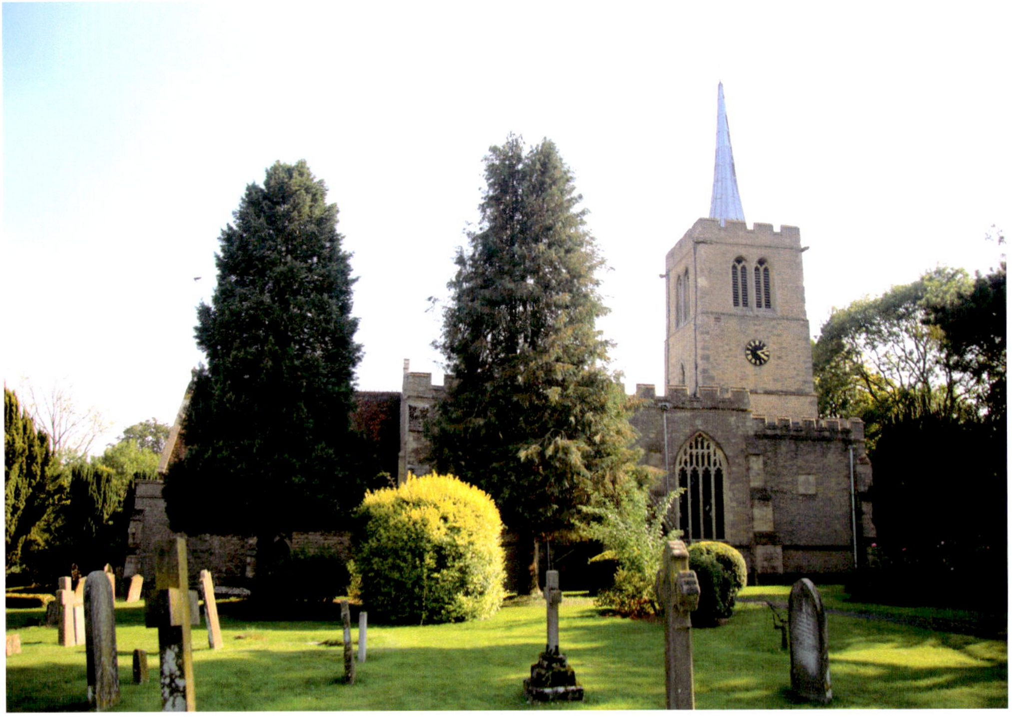

Wootton Church.

Nearby Wootton Manor, which included the site of the present Wootton House, was the home of the Monoux family. These local Baronets were known to be Members of Parliament with family memorials in the form of chancel tablets to be found in the church.

Also worthy of mention is the contemporary piscina in the south wall of the chancel, a reminder of the Catholic Church legacy for cleansing the chalice during Mass.